He Cares for You

Corrie ten Boom

Guideposts®

CARMEL, NEW YORK 10512

www.guidepostsbooks.com

This Guideposts edition is published by special arrangement with
Revell, a division of Baker Book House Company.

© 1978 by Corrie ten Boom
© 1982 by Christians Incorporated

Published by Fleming H. Revell
a division of Baker Book House Company
P.O. Box 6287, Grand Rapids, MI 49516-6287

Previously published as *Don't Wrestle, Just Nestle* (published by Fleming H. Revell in 1978) and *Clippings from My Notebook: Writings and Sayings Collected by Corrie ten Boom* (published by Thomas Nelson in 1982).

Printed in the United States of America

Library of Congress Cataloging-in-Publication Data
Ten Boom, Corrie.
    [Don't wrestle, just nestle]
    He cares for you / Corrie ten Boom.
      p. cm.
    First work originally published: Don't wrestle, just nestle. Old Tappan, N.J. : Revell, c1978. 2nd work originally published: Clippings from my notebook. Nashville : T. Nelson, c1982.
      ISBN 0-8007-1755-4 (cloth)
      1. Christian life—Reformed authors. I. Ten Boom, Corrie. Clippings from my notebook. II. Title. III. Title: Clippings from my notebook.
    BV4501.2.T38 1998
    248.4—dc21   97-38492

Scripture quotations identified KJV are from the King James Version of the Bible.

Scripture quotations identified NASB are from the NEW AMERICAN STANDARD BIBLE ®. Copyright © The Lockman Foundation 1960, 1962, 1963, 1968, 1971, 1972, 1973, 1975. Used by permission.

Scripture quotations identified PHILLIPS are from The New Testament in Modern English (revised edition), translated by J. B. Phillips. © J. B. Phillips 1958, 1960, 1972. Used by permission of Macmillan Publishing Co., Inc.

Scripture quotations identified RSV are from the Revised Standard Version of the Bible, copyright 1946, 1952, 1971 by the Division of Christian Education of the National Council of the Churches of Christ in the USA. Used by permission.

Scripture quotations identified TLB are from *The Living Bible* © 1971. Used by permission of Tyndale House Publishers, Inc., Wheaton, IL 60189. All rights reserved.

Poem by Annie Johnson Flint is used by permission. Evangelical Publishers, Toronto, Canada.

For current information about all releases from Baker Book House, visit our Web site: www.bakerbooks.com

Interior design by Holly Johnson
Front cover design by Cathy Kovacs/Enterprise Four
Back cover design by Dennis Arnold
Typeset by Composition Technologies, Inc.

Contents

Foreword

⸺❦⸺

Corrie ten Boom, the youngest of four children, was born on April 15, 1892, in Amsterdam, the Netherlands. Her father, Casper ten Boom, was a watchmaker, and when Corrie was still a baby, the family moved to Haarlem, where he inherited the family watchshop. Her godly and loving parents reflected the love of the heavenly Father, and when Corrie was five years old she accepted Jesus Christ as her Savior and Lord. She witnessed for Him and prayed for the conversion of those in her neighborhood all through her childhood years.

The ten Boom family home above the watchshop at Barteljorisstraat 19 (called Beje, pronounced "bay-yay," for short) had wide open doors to everybody and especially to those who were in need. Apart from Mr. and Mrs. ten Boom and the four children, the little home was shared by three aunts and later by a succession of foster children.

Corrie became the first woman to be a licensed watchmaker in the Netherlands, but she always said that she never became an expert at it because she was constantly busy with the carrying out of many plans. There were, for example, the clubs she ran—for boys and girls and for mentally retarded children and adults—and a

Christian girl scout movement that eventually comprised thousands of members throughout the Netherlands, Indonesia, and the Dutch Antilles.

In 1844, an unusual event for that time took place. Casper ten Boom's grandfather started a prayer meeting in the Beje for the Jewish people. The ten Boom family loved the Jews, and when Casper ten Boom became involved in hiding and rescuing some of them during the Second World War, he replied, on being warned of the danger involved, "If I die in prison, it will be an honor to have given my life for God's ancient people." He did give his life for them. He and all his children were betrayed and arrested. He died, aged eighty-four, after ten days of imprisonment. Corrie and Betsie, her sister, were transported to Ravensbrück concentration camp, where, after many privations in "the deepest hell that man can create" but with a radiant testimony to the love of God, Betsie died in December 1944. Corrie was released a short time afterward through a clerical error.

After her release, Corrie dedicated her life to telling others what she and Betsie had learned in Ravensbrück: "There is no pit so deep that the love of Jesus Christ is not deeper still." Corrie brought this message to sixty-four countries during thirty-three years of travel. An important part of her message was that when God tells us to forgive our enemies, He gives us the strength and love with which to obey.

I first met Tante Corrie ("aunt" in Dutch) when she was in her seventies, and one of the things that greatly impressed me was her desire to get to know and serve the Lord Jesus better. She was willing to learn from old and young, rich and poor, intellectual and uneducated. Once while attending a funeral with her I saw her making copious notes of the message, which a young minister was giving. Later I became her coworker and traveled with her for a while. Her notebook was always handy. When in 1977 she made her home in California, one of the first things she did was to send for the large pile of notebooks, which, one by one, had accompanied her through the years. How she enjoyed going through them. Through her magazine, The Hiding Place, she passed on to her prayer partners "clippings from her notebook." We now pass these on to you. It was Corrie's prayer that through these writings and favorite Scripture verses Christ would be glorified.

Pamela Rosewell-Moore

1

<hr>

Prescription for Anxiety

This century has been called the Age of Anxiety. How fitting that description is! Everywhere I go, I find people tormented by inner tensions, nervous strain, worries, and fears. We are a generation of worriers, always taking pills to cure our anxieties and relax our nerves.

There is a great deal of difference between worry and concern, and we must realize this. Concern makes us do something to ease the situation. It moves us to take constructive action. But worry burdens our minds and bodies without helping us to find a solution to the problem. Worry is like racing the engine of an automobile without letting in the clutch. You burn energy, but you don't go anywhere.

No doctor has a cure for worry. Oh, he can give you an aspirin for your headache or something for your nervous stomach. He may even give you one pill for your tensions and another pill for your insomnia. But these are not cures. They just cover up the real problem.

There is a permanent cure for worry. The prescription is not mine—it was given by Jesus almost two thousand years ago in His Sermon on the Mount. He devoted a great deal of this talk to the problem of anxiety. Therefore, here is His prescription for anxiety.

Remember the Power of God

A few weeks before the Sermon on the Mount, Jesus walked along the shore of the Sea of Galilee and called twelve men to lay down their fishing nets and follow Him. They would be His disciples. The men saw the presence of God in Jesus. They wanted to follow Him, but still, they had questions—many questions.

"If we don't fish for a living, how will we support our families?"

"How can we be fishers of men? We're afraid to talk to other people."

"How can we carry the gospel to the world? Just the thought of doing that fills us with fear!"

Jesus went up on a mountain to escape the huge crowd that kept following Him. When He was in a private place, He sat down, gathering His disciples around Him. He began to teach them about the kingdom of God. The disciples, who had followed Jesus for a little while now, knew He had no money of His own. Yet He never worried. He seemed content.

"What is the secret of happiness?" they asked.

Jesus replied:

Don't worry about living—wondering what you are going to eat or drink, or what you are going to wear. Surely life is more important than food, and the body more important than the clothes you wear. Look at the birds in the sky. They never sow nor reap nor store away in barns, and yet your Heavenly Father feeds them. Aren't you much more valuable to him than they are? Can any of you, however much he worries, make himself an inch taller? And why do you worry about clothes? Consider how the wild flowers grow. They neither work nor weave, but I tell you that even Solomon in all his glory was not arrayed like one of these! Now if God so clothes the flowers of the field, which are alive today and burned in the stove tomorrow, is he not much more likely to clothe you, you "little-faiths"?

So don't worry and don't keep saying, "What shall we eat, what shall we drink or what shall we wear?" That is what pagans are always looking for; your Heavenly Father knows that you need them all. Set your heart on his kingdom and his goodness, and all these things will come to you as a matter of course.

Don't worry at all then about tomorrow. Tomorrow can take care of itself! One day's trouble is enough for one day.

Matthew 6:25–34 PHILLIPS

Actually, Jesus was chiding them a bit, saying, "You already have life and a body, and they are far more important than what to eat and wear. Does it not follow that the God who is capable of making a human body is capable of putting clothes on it and providing food to keep it going?"

The next time you find yourself depressed or worried about some big problem, remember the power of God. Remember His great miracle of bringing you into being, and you will know He is more than able to care for you.

I remember reading a story about Bishop Quayle, who must have had a keen sense of humor. He told of a time when he sat up late in his study, worrying over many things. Finally the Lord came to him and said, "Quayle, you go to bed. *I'll* sit up the rest of the night."

A friend of mine told me, "When I worry, I go to the mirror and say to myself, 'This tremendous thing that worries me is beyond solution. It is even too hard for God to handle.' And then I smile."

Remember the Foolishness of Worry

Jesus had a way of asking embarrassing questions. "Which of you by taking thought can add one inch to your height?" Can you worry yourself taller? Or shorter? You might worry yourself dead, but never will you worry yourself happier. That comes by a different method.

Alcoholics Anonymous has sound advice to offer their people—advice all of us could use—in the prayer, "O God, give us serenity to accept what cannot be changed, courage to change what should be changed, and wisdom to distinguish the one from the other."

I like that, for there are two things we should not worry about: the things we can change (we need to get busy and do something about these) and the things we cannot change (no amount of worry will help these). Instead, we should let God give us the courage and strength to master the unavoidable, for with God, nothing is impossible.

"Don't be fools; be wise: make the most of every opportunity you have for doing good. Don't act thoughtlessly, but try to find out and do whatever the Lord wants you to do" (Ephesians 5:16–17 TLB).

Jesus says that God is concerned about us personally. "Look at the birds of the air," Jesus said to His disciples. "God feeds them in spite of the fact they cannot drive a tractor, plough a field, or work a harvesting machine.

They can't even build barns to store the grain. Yet God takes care of each one of them." Then He turned to His disciples, and I imagine He had a slight smile on His face. "Are you not of more value than they?"

Next Jesus pointed to the wild flowers that were poking their heads around the rocks in the hard soil of Israel. "Look at them," He said. "They can't run a spindle or loom; they don't even have the ability to sit down at a sewing machine and make their own clothes. But see how beautifully God has dressed them. Why? Because God cares for even the grass of the field." Then He said, "If God so clothes the grass of the field, will He not much more clothe you?" (see Matthew 6:25–30).

Count Your Blessings

I was in Japan, very tired, with a stomach that was upset from the unusual food. How I longed for a good European meal, a table where I would not have to sit cross-legged on the floor, and a soft bed instead of the hard mats the Japanese sleep on. I was filled with self-pity. I wanted to be back in Holland!

That night in church, while I was busy feeling sorry for myself, I saw a man in a wheelchair. After the service my interpreter took me down to meet the man, a bent little fellow with yellow skin and slender hands. His face wore the happiest expression I could imagine.

"What are those little packets on your lap?" I asked the man, pointing to several packages wrapped in brown paper and tied with string.

He broke into a wide grin and tenderly unwrapped one of the packages. It was a sheath of pages covered with

Braille, the raised script of the blind. "This is the Gospel of John, written in Braille. I have just finished it," he said.

Then he continued. "This is the fifteenth time I have written the Gospel of John in Braille. I have also written other of the Gospels, as well as many shorter portions of the Bible."

"How did you come to do this?"

"Do you know about the Bible women here in Japan?" he asked. "Bible women go from village to village, bringing copies of the Bible, books, and literature to those who are hungry for God. Our Bible woman is very ill with tuberculosis, but she travels every week to sixteen villages, even though she will soon die. When I heard about it, I asked the Lord what I could do to help her.

"Although my legs are paralyzed, and I cannot get out of the wheelchair, in many ways I am healthier than she. God showed me that though her hands are shaky and my legs paralyzed, I could be the hands, and she the legs. I punch out the pages of Braille, and she takes the Bibles around to the villages and gives them to the blind people, who miss so much because they cannot see."

I left the church that night filled not with self-pity, but with shame. Here was I, with two good legs for traveling all over the world, two good lungs, and two good eyes, complaining because I didn't like the food!

These precious people had discovered a sure cure for self-pity—service to others. Perhaps it is like the slogan I once saw on a church sign in America. "If you are unhappy with your lot in life, build a service station on it." The best antidote I know for self-pity is to help someone else who is worse off than you.

"I complained that I had no shoes, then I saw a man who had no legs, and I stopped complaining."

Walk with God

Does the Lord Jesus say, "Come along now. Take it easy. Don't worry," leaving us to realize that there have never been so many reasons to worry as there are now?

No! The Lord gives an answer.

"Seek first his kingdom and his righteousness" (see Matthew 6:33). It is your relationship with your heavenly Father that is important. That is what determines whether you will be victorious or defeated, however difficult the circumstances are.

The day after He fed the five thousand, Jesus chastised the crowd that followed Him, accusing them of following Him because He had fed them. "But you shouldn't be so concerned about perishable things like food. No, spend your energy seeking the eternal life that I, the Messiah, can give you. For God the Father has sent me for this very purpose" (John 6:27 TLB).

Still the crowd was more concerned with food. They asked Him to give them free bread every day, as Moses did in the desert. Jesus told them, "Moses didn't give it to them. My Father did. And now he offers you true Bread from heaven. The true Bread is a Person—the one sent by God from heaven, and he gives life to the world" (John 6:32–33 TLB).

The crowd, still not understanding what Jesus was telling them, asked that they might have every day the bread He was describing.

"I am the Bread of Life. No one coming to me will ever be hungry again. Those believing in me will never thirst," Jesus told them (John 6:35 TLB). Although He said this over and over again to the crowd, they still failed to understand or accept. Many of His disciples left Him at this point. Jesus then turned and asked the twelve if they, too, were leaving Him.

Simon Peter answered for all of them: "Master, to whom shall we go? You alone have the words that give eternal life, and we believe them and know you are the holy Son of God" (John 6:68–69 TLB). Peter and the others who stayed with Jesus knew what was important and what was not. They knew the way to victory.

With your hand in the Father's hand, you stand on victory ground. Give room for the Holy Spirit. He gives you the right outlook on troubling events. I know that from the time that I saw my sister Betsie starving in a prison camp. We were surrounded by people who had behind them a training in cruelties, but we had moments when we were conscious that we were walking with the Lord.

Often we had to go too early to roll call, which started at 3:30 A.M. Betsie and I would walk through the camp, and there were three of us present. Betsie said something, I said something, and the Lord said something. I can't tell you how, but both Betsie and I understood clearly what He said. These walks were a bit of heaven in the midst of hell. Everything around us was black and dark, but in us there was a light that belonged to eternity.

Jesus said:

All who listen to my instructions and follow them are wise, like a man who builds his house on solid rock. Though the rain comes in torrents, and the floods rise and the storm winds beat against his house, it won't collapse, for it is built on rock.

Matthew 7:24–25 TLB

2

No Time for Anxiety

Our fears for today, our worries about tomorrow, or where we are—high above the sky, or in the deepest ocean—nothing will ever be able to separate us from the love of God demonstrated by our Lord Jesus Christ when he died for us" (Romans 8:38–39 TLB). We were in Africa. Prisoners were dancing. The pounding rhythm created an atmosphere of demonical darkness. The expressions of the dancers' faces made me afraid. It was as though they were dancing themselves into a trance, possessed by dark powers. Their shouting influenced the other dancers, causing the gloomy darkness in their eyes to increase every minute.

These people were criminals. They knew what it was to be inspired by hell itself. Next to me were three black Christian brothers, who had accompanied me to this place hidden far away in the jungle—the place where I was to speak. We waited for the prison director to join us.

At last he came. He was a friendly man, but I could see that he knew how to make people obey. "I am so glad you came to speak to my men." He clapped his hands and shouted, "Stop dancing! Sit down and listen to what Miss ten Boom has to tell you."

I saw the anger flash in their eyes. It was hard for these men to part from the spirits who had kept them in their power. About four hundred men settled down in front of me, and about two hundred were standing behind me. I saw not one friendly face among the six hundred. I looked at my three black Christian brothers and felt uneasy that not one white man had accompanied me. I underestimated those men badly, as I later clearly discovered.

I softly prayed, "Lord, I know that those who are with me are more and stronger than those who are against me. Let Your never-failing love fill my heart and mouth, and also the man who will interpret for me."

I spoke rather a long time to those prisoners, and I saw the expressions on their faces change as they heard me say, "Jesus loved *you* when He died on the cross for the sins of the whole world." I never saw such a dramatic change in people. They came from darkness into light— from the darkness of hell into the light of heaven.

As we waited at the gate while a guard found the key, a prisoner came running toward me. He took my hand and said something. My interpreter translated, "You came to us because God's love is in you. Thank you. Thank Him!"

We squeezed into the tiny car and headed down the primitive path through the jungle, going toward Kampala. The moment we got into the car, my three brothers began to sing and praise the Lord. I was sitting in the front seat, squeezed against the driver. The other two men were crowded into the tiny backseat. But even our cramped positions did not keep them from singing and praising God as we roared through the dense jungle.

What a strange sight we must have been, bouncing down the jungle road, weaving from side to side to miss the holes and puddles, singing and praising the Lord in loud voices!

I saw a man ahead, standing on the side of the narrow

road. He had the tire and wheel from a car leaning against his leg. The driver slowed the car to a stop and shouted across me, "What is the matter, my friend?"

"Please bring me to Kampala," he pleaded. "My tire is flat, and my wheel is broken."

What a pity we have no room, I thought.

But my happy black brothers saw no such problem. "Of course," they shouted together. "Join us. We like to help our brothers in the name of Jesus."

The man came around to the other side of the car, to get into the front seat between the driver and me. While he was walking around, one of the men in the backseat leaned forward and whispered. "Pray with us, Tante Corrie, that we bring him to the Lord before we reach Kampala."

How they squeezed him in, I'll never know. But soon we were on our way again, the man jammed between the driver and me holding that big, rusty car wheel and the dirty black tire on his lap. The men in the car began singing and praising the Lord again, keeping time with the bumps in the road.

The driver began to talk to the man in his own language, and the other men enthusiastically entered in. I could not understand what they were saying, but I knew they were talking to him about the Lord Jesus. I prayed, keeping my eyes on the road.

Suddenly the passenger looked at the driver and said something. One of the men in the backseat interpreted for me. The passenger was asking if he knew the driver. Hadn't they met before?

"Sure," the driver answered. "Last year you and I were in the same prison, where we have just been with Miss ten Boom. You know, boy, at that time I served the devil.

Now I serve Jesus Christ. He uses me to save lives of other sinners, and He will use you from now on also."

The man with the big wheel in his lap listened intently. Before long, he accepted Jesus as his Savior. I wanted to join in the men's praises, but I was too concerned about the road and the wild way in which the driver was swerving from side to side. *Surely we'll all be killed*, I worried.

Then, ahead, we saw a woman with two children waiting alongside the road. "Let us give her a lift and also bring her to Jesus," one of the men shouted.

Did he really mean it? There was absolutely no room!

The car stopped, and for a minute I entertained the hope that they were just going to witness to her where she was and drive on. But no, they motioned her to join us in the car!

As she got in the backseat with her two children, I saw a third come out from under her coat. Somehow they all got in, sitting on top of one another. One of the small children had to crawl over my shoulder and sit on my lap. I could not feel my legs. Never, never had I been in such an overcrowded automobile—and on such a terrible road.

We started up again, the car rolling from right to left, left to right, bouncing off rocks and logs alongside the road, weaving over shaky jungle bridges. But the black men were tremendously happy, believing the Lord had put the woman there so they could pick her up and witness to her. This time, all four of the men—including the one with the big wheel on his lap—eagerly joined in the conversation, telling the woman about the Lord Jesus Christ.

Suddenly the four men began to sing "Tuku tenderesa Jesu," an African song of praise. The woman had accepted Jesus as her Savior and Lord.

We arrived in Kampala and swerved through the traffic, the men still singing and banging their hands against the side of the automobile in time with the music. Our fellow travelers left us—the man with the big wheel and the woman with her three children—but not until my friends had obtained their names so they could follow up their work. Then they took me to the place I was staying.

After they had gone, I sat for a long time, rubbing life back into my legs and trying to get some insight into the events of the afternoon. While I, the cautious European, had been so anxious and worried about the fierce prison, the horrible road, the old car, and the discomforts and dangers of the trip, my black brothers had no time for anxiety. They were too busy praising God and sharing the good news with those whom God sent into their path. They did not see the people along the road as problems but as opportunities.

Perhaps, I thought, as I lay back on the bed to rest my aching body, if I would spend less time worrying whether the car would run, the road was paved, or the bridges would hold—and lose myself in praise and service as these African brothers did—I would not only live longer but more abundantly. While I was anxious about reaching my destination, they were excited about meeting people along the way. Reaching the destination seemed almost incidental to praising God and serving Him as they went.

Maybe the way in which we travel and the attitude we have while making our way through life is more important than reaching our destination. Or could it be that, in God's sight, the way actually is the destination?

Jesus said, "I am the Way—yes, and the Truth and the Life" (John 14:6 TLB).

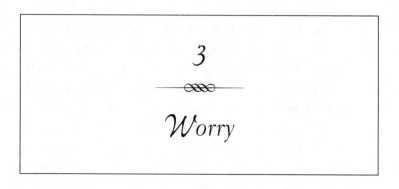

3

Worry

"**D**on't worry over anything whatever; tell God
every detail of your needs in earnest and thankful
prayer, and the peace of God, which transcends human
understanding, will keep constant guard over your
hearts and minds as they rest in Christ Jesus"
(Philippians 4:6 PHILLIPS).

Before the battle, the general always sends his spies into
the enemy camp. They take photographs of secret defenses,
they learn the enemy's battle positions, their ammunition
supply points, even the personal weaknesses of the oppos-
ing leaders. But unless the general passes this information
on to his own troops, they cannot win the battle.

That is why I want to share with you some of the
things I have learned about the enemy and about the
Victor, Jesus Christ. I want you to know that God expects
us to be conquerors over the powers of darkness—not
only for the sake of our personal victory and for the liberation of others who are in bondage to Satan, but for His
glory. He wants the world to know that He is triumphant
and victorious, and the only way it will ever know is by
our demonstration of God's power and authority.

Once a man saved up his money for years and bought
the house of his dreams. It was in the countryside, with

mountains and streams all around it. He could not wait to begin living in his new house, but because of his business, he could not move in for several months. So he allowed the man who was living there to stay as a caretaker until he was ready to move in himself.

But when the new owner came to move into his dream house, the other man said, "No, I am staying here. You find somewhere else to live."

"But you promised you would move out when I was ready," the owner said.

The man gave a laugh and replied, "This is my home. You cannot come in." Then he slammed the door in the owner's face and locked it.

The owner marched straight to the police station with his papers of ownership. The next time he knocked on the door of his house, there were two large policemen standing next to him. When the man in the house saw the policemen, he meekly packed his belongings and left the house to its owner.

What the true owner of the house could not do in his own strength, he was able to do when he appeared with authority on his side. It is the same with us. Satan may laugh at us and continue to afflict us with disease, fear, anxiety, and defeat. But when we come to him in the name of Jesus, he knows we have all the authority of the kingdom of God behind us, and he must flee.

Worry Is Sin

I had to learn that worry is sin before I could get rid of the worry. First I tried to "fear not" as an act of obedience. It was as successful as trying to kill a lion with a toy gun. Then I began to learn the secrets. First you must ask forgiveness for your sin of worry. Then you need to accept the cleansing of the blood of Jesus. Finally, you need to let God fill you with the Holy Spirit. When you are filled with the Holy Spirit, the spirit of fear will flee, forced out by power and love and a sound mind.

In the latter part of 1946, a group of Christian ladies in Ottawa asked me to give my testimony at an evening meeting.

I did not even know where I would sleep that night, but I went in obedience. I felt it was a training in trusting God. How good that the coach was the Lord Himself!

It was the first time that I had been in Canada. I remember that the spirit of worry was very busy with me. Sometimes my traveling went smoothly. God gave me friends who organized my meetings, and I went where He told me to go. But now I was not quite sure of the Lord's guidance. At such moments I felt far from Holland. A big ocean was between my hometown and me.

So often that tramp for the Lord, the prisoner Paul, had helped me. I opened my Bible and read what he wrote from his prison in Rome: "Be careful for nothing; but in every thing by prayer and supplication with thanksgiving let your requests be made known unto God. And the peace of God, which passeth all understanding, shall keep your hearts and minds through Christ Jesus" (Philippians 4:6–7 KJV).

My, but Paul knew about worry! Still, he found the answer: "I can do all things through Christ which strengtheneth me" (Philippians 4:13 KJV).

I did not even know where I would sleep that night, but God had used Paul to encourage me, and I trusted Him.

That evening, I told my problem to the dear people

who heard my talk, and sure enough, a lady came to me and said, "You are very welcome in my home. I have a small guest room you may use." I had been worried about finding a place to sleep, but the Lord had the answer all worked out for me!

What a joy to be surrounded by kind people. Before I fell asleep, I thought of the time shortly before, when enemies were all around me, and how they hated me because of what I had done for the Jews. Soon I was sound asleep.

Suddenly the light in my room came on. I opened my eyes, and a uniformed officer was standing in front of me. My only thought was, *This is the Gestapo. They have found me.* I said to the man, "I am not a Jew." Then I remembered where I was and told him that I was a guest of the lady of the house. Without a word, the man put the light out and left.

What had happened? He was the owner of the house and had come home late. He did not want his wife to see him at that hour, especially since he had been drinking too much that night. He decided to go to the guest room, but his plan misfired because of my presence there. When he told his wife, she was very disturbed. What a shock it must have been for her guest! She put on her robe and ran to my room. There she found me, fast asleep!

Some months later, I met my host again. It was a bitterly cold evening. I had spoken that afternoon in a town some distance from Ottawa, where I was to speak in the evening. Friends had brought me to a house halfway between the two towns, and my former host was waiting there. He told me that he was going to take me to Ottawa, where the meeting was to start at 8:00 P.M.

The highway was so icy that we skidded from right to left. I looked at my friend and saw that he had given himself courage for the drive by taking some drinks, and it was not a little amount that he had enjoyed. I thought about the coming evening. How could I sit for hours in that car, worrying about the slippery road and his driving, and then still have the power to speak? I couldn't. I was worried—I thought I had reason to be—but I knew that my worry was a sin. I would have to ask forgiveness for my sin and trust the Lord to deliver us safely to Ottawa.

I prayed for strength and then said to the driver, "Jim, I am going to speak tonight, and it is impossible for me to worry for several hours beforehand, while you skid from right to left and left to right. So I hope you don't mind, but I am going to sleep."

Jim smiled and said, "You go ahead. I will drive and not sleep." And he did. The Lord gave me a very good rest.

The young girl who was my secretary at that time was sitting behind me, and she told me later that I snored all the way. That was a comfort to her, because she knew that I was not worried, but she said it was still the most terrible car ride of her life. We arrived safely, on time for the evening meeting, and I was refreshed and ready for my talk.

God's Armor

The battle always has to be fought before the victory is won, though many people think they must have the victory *before* the battle. The conflict with worry and fear is almost always there—each person must overcome or be overcome. But we must fight each battle of our lives in the strength of Jesus' victory. He said, "As the Father has sent me, even so I am sending you" (John 20:21 TLB). We are to be like Jesus—One of whom Satan is afraid!

When we worry, we are carrying tomorrow's load with today's strength; carrying two days in one. We are moving into tomorrow ahead of time. There is just one day in the calendar of action—today. The Holy Spirit does not give a clear blueprint of our whole lives, but only of the moments, one by one.

We all have the same enemies—we are all preyed upon by frustration and worry. In India, Australia, Japan, Germany—we need the same Holy Spirit. We need to remember that we are children of God, living within His constant care. God knows and is interested both in the hardest problems we face and the tiniest details that concern us. He knows how to put everything in place, like a jigsaw puzzle, to make a beautiful picture.

But Satan has a very good secret service. The moment you step out from under God's umbrella of grace, you are discovered and attacked by Satan. Recognition of Satan's attack is half the fight. An attacking enemy who is not recognized already has half his battle won. Never knowing where, how, and when Satan will attack us, we should never be unprotected or unprepared. We need to be clothed with the whole armor of God.

> Last of all I want to remind you that your strength must come from the Lord's mighty power within you. Put on all of God's armor so that you will be able to stand safe against all strategies and tricks of Satan. So use every piece of God's armor to resist the enemy whenever he attacks, and when it is all over, you will still be standing up.
>
> *Ephesians 6:10–11, 13 TLB*

What a relief to know that we do not need to provide the armor! God makes the armor—we just put it on. But the armor has no protection for the back, for God does not expect any deserters. Neither is the armor a museum piece—it is given for use on the battlefield. Jesus is Victor!

Every temptation to worry or fear is an opportunity for victory. It is a signal to fly the flag of our Victor. It is the chance to make the tempter know anew that he is defeated.

> Thine, O LORD, is the greatness, and the power, and the glory, and the victory, and the majesty: for all that is in the heaven and in the earth is thine; thine is the kingdom, O LORD, and thou art exalted as head above all. Both riches and honour come of thee, and thou reignest over all; and in thine hand is power and might; and in thine hand it is to make great, and to give strength unto all.
>
> *1 Chronicles 29:11–12* KJV

4

―――⦿⦿⦿⦿⦿――――

May a Christian Worry?

Why, therefore should we do ourselves this wrong,
Or others—that we are not always strong,
That we are ever overborne with care,
That we should ever weak and heartless be,
Anxious or troubled, when with us is prayer,
And joy and strength and courage are with Thee.

Author Unknown

We imagine that a little anxiety and worry are indications of how wise we are. We think we see the dangers of life clearly. In reality, however, our fears are only an indication of how wicked we really are.

As Charles G. Trumbull says:

Worry is sin; a black, murderous, God-defying, Christ-rejecting sin; worry about anything, at any time whatever. We will never know victory over worry and anxiety until we begin to treat it as sin. For such it is. It is a deep-seated distrust of the Father, who assures us again and again that even the falling sparrow is in His tender care.

The words *fear not* occur many times in the Bible. The Word of God has no suggestions; only commandments.

So if we fear and worry, we are being disobedient, and disobedience is always a sin.

The only way blunders and destruction can occur in our lives is when we forget to trust God. When we take things into our own unskilled hands, we get everything knotted and tangled.

Worry is utterly useless. It never serves a good purpose. It brings no good results. One cannot think or see clearly when worrying. Let pagans worry, if they will, but we must not, for we have a living Savior, our Lord Jesus Christ, and His conquering power. His victory can be our victory. Life at best is brief, and there is so much to be accomplished. If we must burn ourselves out, let us burn out for God.

In this age of increasing pace, it is so easy to follow the crowd and let materialism become our god. But if we do, only too often we find that worry and tension become our masters. The effects of tension are seen in all spheres of life. Tension leads to inefficiency and frayed nerves with our fellow workers and students. In politics, it leads to strain in international relations and fears of war. In the home, tension leads to irritability with our husband or wife, destroying the very thing God meant to be perfect.

For with people who are not content, worry has a fair chance. Paul writes:

> I have learned to be content, whatever the circumstances may be. I know now how to live when things are difficult and I know how to live when things are prosperous. In general and in particular I have learned the secret . . . of facing either plenty or poverty. I am ready for anything through the strength of the one who lives within me.
>
> *Philippians 4:11–13* PHILLIPS

Lonely Contentment

I have never been so poor as the time that I was in solitary confinement. How difficult it was to learn to be content. But Paul wrote once, while in prison, that we are God's workmanship. I experienced the same. The lessons were difficult, but the Teacher was so powerful. The Lord was my all-sufficiency. I wrote home: "The Lord Jesus is everything to me. He never leaves me alone. I concentrate on the Savior. With Him there is certainty, with the other things, only uncertainty and delayed hope, which hurts the heart. Once I asked to be freed, but the Lord said, 'My grace is sufficient for you.'"

That brought my thoughts to Paul. He had to learn a lesson. Three times he asked the Lord to take away the thorn in the flesh (see 2 Corinthians 12:8). Then he got this answer: God's grace was sufficient for him. That was true for Paul and it was true for me. In a way I knew that there was a danger that the joy I felt and my security in Him would lose some of their power when I was free; when the securities of the world would once again be a comfortable foundation to rest upon.

When the Lord gives you the ability, through His grace, to accept the situation, that contentment can help you to get rid of your worry, whatever happens. But could I ever accept being a prisoner alone in a cell? I surely could not, but Paul told about all grace, always, in all things (see 2 Corinthians 9:8).

Once when I was in the cell, I heard the bolt on the outside of my door being undone. A guard opened the door and commanded, "Follow me!" I was being called out to be questioned. It was the first time I had left the cell during that lonely imprisonment. Yes, lonely—night and day I was alone. First we had to go through long corridors with cell doors on both sides, then through a door that opened onto the outside. I breathed deeply. I was in a courtyard. The walk was almost too short to the small barracks where people were questioned. I looked up to the sky, then around me, and then down and saw blades of grass and some tiny white flowers. The little flower "Shepherd's purse" was growing between the bricks used to pave the courtyard.

When the guard who accompanied me looked the other way, I quickly bent over and picked some of those little flowers and hid them inside my dress. When back in my cell, I took a broken medicine bottle, arranged my bouquet, and put it behind my cup so that the guards could not see it when they looked through the peephole in my door. That tiny bouquet was my garden, and I enjoyed it as the only nice thing in my cell.

I was ready to accept my little bouquet of six blades of grass and three little flowers as my garden because of Him who was in me, and I could say then with Paul, "I look upon everything as loss compared with the over-whelming gain of knowing Christ Jesus my Lord. For his sake I did in actual fact suffer the loss of everything, but I considered it useless rubbish compared with being able to win Christ" (Philippians 3:8 PHILLIPS).

Demon Influence

When we are worrying, we are not trusting. Yet we who have burdens and responsibilities are inclined to worry. Again, it is so important that we recognize the enemy. Worry and depression are sister and brother. I want to tell you about something that I experienced—a time when the influence of depression was practically nationwide.

After I was released from the German concentration camp, I returned to Holland until the war was over. Then God told me to go back to Germany, to carry the good news of Christ's victory over fear and guilt. When I arrived in Germany, however, I found the people in great confusion. Many German people had beloved relatives missing. Were they still in Russian concentration camps? Had they died in battle or in the horrible bombings? This uncertainty drove many people to desperation.

Many of these people were turning to the fortune-tellers to find their answers. While the evil spirits, working through the fortune-tellers, often gave just enough accurate information to keep the people coming back, something else also happened. Many of those who visited the fortune-tellers later developed horrible fears, depression, and anxiety. Their hearts, it seemed, were always in the gloom of darkness. They often had the urge to commit suicide. I immediately recognized this as sure evidence of demon influence.

Jesus said, "I am the Light of the world. So if you follow me, you won't be stumbling through the darkness, for living light will flood your path" (John 8:12 TLB). Even if a child of God has visited a fortune-teller and come under demon influence, he does not have to remain in darkness. He can be set free.

Realizing this, I began speaking against the sins of the occult. It was the occult that was putting people in bondage, causing them to break down mentally and spiritually. I often read Deuteronomy 18:10–13 to point out how these sins are an abomination in the sight of God. Instead of depending on God's power, the people were rushing to the enemy for help. And as we know, the enemy is a liar, whose very purpose is to deceive people and lead them away from the truth.

I showed the German Christians how Jesus Christ has provided an answer to this serious problem. Satan is not the Victor, Jesus is. And even if the people had invited the demons in, Christ could overcome that. They did not have to live with their depression or fear any more. They had to be set free. I was able to say to them:

> [God] gave you a share in the very life of Christ, for he forgave all your sins, and blotted out the charges proved against you, the list of his commandments which you had not obeyed. He took this list of sins and destroyed it by nailing it to Christ's cross. In this way God took away Satan's power to accuse you of sin, and God openly displayed to the whole world Christ's triumph at the cross where your sins were all taken away.
>
> *Colossians* 2:13–15 TLB

In the Old Testament there is an interesting story of the lost axhead. A son of the prophets had been chopping wood, and his axhead had fallen into the Jordan River. Since it was a borrowed ax, he was worried and afraid. He ran to Elisha for help. Elisha sent him back to the place where he had made his mistake, so the miracle of restoration could happen. The axhead floated to the surface, the young man grabbed it and replaced it on the handle (see 2 Kings 6:1–6).

Just so, you need to go back to the place where you opened the door of your life to the influence of the spirit of worry. Where did the fear enter? What was it that caused you to start worrying? Remember, the spirit of fear does not come from God. Instead, God gives us power and love and a sound mind (see 2 Timothy 1:7). Therefore, you need to ask the Lord Jesus to close the door that you opened.

How is this done? First you need to recognize that you have sinned. Most fear, anxiety, and worry come through the sin of not trusting God.

Second, confession is necessary. Face yourself. Tell God. And then, if possible, confess to someone close to you. When all of this is done, you may then claim the precious promises for cleansing. You will instantly be freed from the bondage of Satan.

Worry is a demon—fear of demons comes from demons themselves. As children of God, we have nothing to fear. He who is with us is much stronger than he who is against us. "And he asked them, 'Why were you so fearful? Don't you even yet have confidence in me?'" (Mark 4:40 TLB).

"The seed among the thorns represents those who listen and believe God's words but whose faith afterwards is choked out by worry and riches and the responsibilities and pleasures of life" (Luke 8:14 TLB).

May we worry? We have a whole Bible as our guide, Jesus Christ as our living Savior who loves us, and heaven as our future!

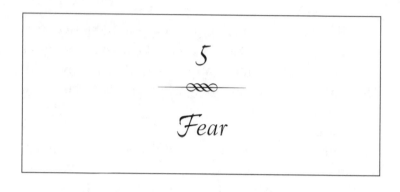

5

Fear

"For God hath not given us the spirit of fear; but of power, and of love, and of a sound mind" (2 Timothy 1:7 KJV). Fear is the atmosphere of worry. Nothing weakens us as much as fear. On the other hand, nothing weakens the tempter as much as a quiet, bold, steady fearlessness. Satan cannot operate in the atmosphere of trust.

Oh, but fear and worry can talk so wisely! You may often think they are right, but fear is often a stupid blunder. Once I worked for a month in Los Angeles during a flu epidemic. One morning my secretary woke up with a bad headache, and I feared she had the flu.

"Girl, please stay in bed. I have to go to a college to speak at nine o'clock, but I will go alone," I told her. Once I was outside, I felt a headache myself. My eyes felt so strange. I knew that headaches and eye problems were sometimes symptoms of the flu, and I worried all the way to the college. I had so much work to do—I didn't have time for the flu!

Once at the college, I opened my Bible to begin my talk and found that I could not read even one letter! Fear whispered, "You have the flu in your eyes." I was not sure that was possible, but I listened to my fear. What would

I do if I could not read? I need to prepare for my talks and to study the Bible, if I am to speak about the Lord. Could I go back to my former trade of watchmaking? Impossible! I would need my eyes more for that than for any other trade.

I know that I did not give a happy talk that morning, for when worry and fear are on the throne, you are not an open channel for streams of living water. It is impossible to listen to the Lord's voice while listening to your own fear. Fear is so loud, so insistent, so time-consuming!

Near the end of my talk, my secretary came quietly into the room and sat down in the back row of the auditorium. When I finished my talk and the students left, I went to her. "Why didn't you stay in bed when you had such a headache?"

"Oh, I am not ill. My headache is gone," she answered.

"All right, but it could have been the beginning of the flu. You should have stayed home and started answering the letters that I gave you."

"That's why I came. I couldn't work, because you have *my* glasses!" Both our glasses had exactly the same frame, but far different lenses! We both laughed at our mistake. My flu had gone. So had my headache. Once we traded glasses, I could read perfectly, and I was ashamed to have listened to my silly, blundering fear all morning.

Trust the Vine

Anxiety, fear, and worry are the result of our unwillingness to trust God. To worry is the same as saying to God, "I don't believe You." Do you fear for your finances? Are you afraid you won't be able to feed or shelter your loved ones? Do you lie awake and fear your fears? Listen to what God says!

"Give your burdens to the Lord. He will carry them. He will not permit the godly to slip or fall" (Psalm 55:22 TLB).

"And it is he [God] who will supply all your needs from his riches in glory, because of what Christ Jesus has done for us" (Philippians 4:19 TLB).

"Stay away from the love of money; be satisfied with what you have. For God has said, 'I will never, *never* fail you nor forsake you.' That is why we can say without any doubt or fear, 'The Lord is my Helper and I am not afraid of anything that mere man can do to me'" (Hebrews 13:5–6 TLB).

Remember when Jesus told the parable of the vine and the branches in John 15? He said the secret to abundant living is in staying attached to the vine. An unattached branch has something to fear. Not only can it not produce fruit, but it will be burned in the fire. But an attached branch has no fears. All it has to do is nestle close to the vine, and the vine does all the work, sending its sap through the branch and producing luscious grapes. It is not the branch that produces the grapes, it is the vine.

"But if you stay in me and obey my commands, you may ask any request you like, and it will be granted! My true disciples produce bountiful harvests. This brings great glory to my Father" (John 15:7–8 TLB).

Fear does not take away the grief of yesterday, nor does it solve the problems of tomorrow. All it does is rob you of the power of today. Rather than wind up on a psychiatrist's couch or an undertaker's slab, do what God tells you. Seek first His kingdom and His righteousness. He will add everything else you need.

Fear or Victory?

There are many people who don't realize that fear is the enemy. When the fight is on and blows are being exchanged, fear is a sure element of defeat. Fear sucks the spirit out of one's fighting, takes the nerve out of one's courage, robs vim and zest from one's action. But this is always a false fear, because it tells us the enemy is stronger than we are. That is not true! We know that Jesus is Victor, and a fear that tells us otherwise is false.

When you become a child of God, you are a target for the enemy, and he will do his utmost to tell you that you are crazy. Sometimes you think that you are not a Christian when you have trouble, but I should very much doubt whether you are a Christian at all if you did *not* have trouble.

The whole of the New Testament and the history of the church show that when we are children of God, we are in a fight of faith. Not having any troubles in your life is therefore far from being a good sign. It is indeed a serious sign that there is something radically wrong. There is a special reason for my saying that, because we are special objects of the attention of the enemy. Why not have problems when it is God's way to bless you!

"Count it all joy when ye fall into divers temptations" (James 1:2 KJV). That is the way your faith is proved. The devil cannot rob us of our salvation, thank God! But he can make us miserable. He can fill us with his false fear.

It is the tempter who knows real fear. His fear is founded on fact and experience. He has met One greater and stronger than himself. Satan is afraid of his Victor. He knows what it means to be thwarted and resisted, beaten back steadily and driven clear off the battleground. There has been a man upon the earth whom Satan fears—whom he can neither trust nor resist—Jesus Christ. He learned to fear Him in Nazareth and in the wilderness. Jesus' absolute, steady obedience to the Father beat Satan. Even the storm on Galilee's blue waters, so unusually violent that it frightened the experienced sailors, failed to touch Jesus with fear.

Fear is as common as sin. If we could be wholly free of fear, we would have stronger bodies, minds, spirits, faith, courage, and power. The tempter continually plays on our sense of fear. For instance, people's fear of being in personal want is holding back huge amounts of money—money which could change the condition of the whole heathen world and move forward the date of Jesus' coming.

At our side there is always conflict with the tempter. Each of us must overcome or be overcome. Our victory comes through Jesus' victory, and we must fight in the strength of His victory. Throw out your self-seeking spirit—it allows Satan a free hand to do as he chooses. Yield to the Holy Spirit. He will burn out your self-spirit.

Men as Trees Walking

In his book *Spiritual Depression: Its Causes and Cure*, Dr. D. Martyn Lloyd-Jones wrote about the great importance of living as rich as we are in Jesus Christ.

> If all Christians simply began to function as the New Testament would have us do, there would be no problem of evangelism. It is because we are failing as Christian people in our daily lives and witness that

the Church counts for so little and so few are attracted to God. So for that most urgent reason alone, it behooves us to deal with this question.

We are like the man who was blind and healed, but still saw men as trees walking (see Mark 8:22–26). Yes, we have received the healing touch from Jesus—we were born again the moment we asked Him to come into our hearts—but people around us are not envious to receive the same. This is simply because we do not behave like happy, fearless people. We have unlimited riches through the promises of the Bible and the presence of the Lord in our hearts, but we still see men as trees walking.

Jesus asked the blind man, "Can you see?"

The man answered, "Not quite one hundred percent, Lord." How good it was that he told the Lord! Jesus gave him another touch of healing, and his eyesight was perfect. I am sure that even if Jesus had not asked him, the man would have told the Lord the problem and been satisfied.

So, if your sight is still only partial, tell the Lord, "Thank You, Lord, for what You did, for what You gave me—but I need more."

For Jesus said, "Blessed are they which do hunger and thirst after righteousness: for they shall be filled" (Matthew 5:6 KJV). He did not tell the blind man, "Try hard to see." The man had only to ask, and it was given to him.

You and I must ask Jesus to do the job through His Holy Spirit. He is the One who makes our eyes to see. "But when the Holy Spirit controls our lives he will produce this kind of fruit in us: love, joy, peace, patience, kindness, goodness, faithfulness, gentleness and self-control" (Galatians 5:22–23 TLB).

We are often too content with a partial healing. I had an experience of liberation from resentment some time ago. Some friends, fine Christian people, had done something really mean against me, and I had forgiven them. That is what I had thought.

A friend asked me how the situation was, but I told him, "I don't want to talk about it. I have forgiven it."

"I understand that," he answered, "but I should like to know what they think about it."

"Oh, they take it easy. They simply say that they have never done it. Perhaps they forget that I have everything in black and white, in the letters which they wrote to me at that time."

My friend looked at me and waited a moment. Then he said: "Where are your sins? You told us in your talk this morning that when we confess our sins, God casts them into the depths of the sea and you even believe that there is a sign saying 'No Fishing Allowed.' But the sins of your friends you have in black and white. 'Lord, I pray that You will give Corrie the grace to burn all the black and white of the sins of others today as a sweet-smelling sacrifice before she goes to bed.'"

I surely did, and how well I slept that night. Now when I meet these people, I enjoy a peace that makes our friendship an unusual joy.

No, it was not easy. As a matter of fact, I needed the Lord just as much as when I had to forgive the people who had been cruel to my family. Forgiving is a hard job. But in 2 Corinthians 9:8 Paul tells us that there is always grace, sufficient for everything. The Holy Spirit taught me a prayer that always helps me: "Thank You, Lord Jesus, that You brought into my heart God's love through the Holy Spirit. Thank You, Father, that Your love in me is stronger than my resentment" (see Romans 5:5).

No compromise. The Lord is willing and able to give us clear sight. When worry gets static, it becomes depression. When unforgiveness is healed, there is a liberation that makes the enemy run.

Have you the black and white of the sins of others? Burn them today. Together with the Lord, you can.

Children of the Light

One time, artists were invited to paint a picture of peace. The pictures were many and varied, but the winner depicted a little bird sitting calmly on her nest, which was built on a slender branch overhanging Niagara Falls. The peace of the little bird did not depend on her surroundings. And so it is with us. As Christians, our peace of heart and freedom from fear do not depend on our circumstances but on our trust in God. Fear is want of faith.

Being a Christian does not mean there is no more battle. It means we have a strategic point of attack in the battle. The battle position of the Christian is victory, joy, and abundance. The Lord expects us to do no more than welcome His assistance. The doors of heaven are open. If I hold on to feelings that prevent me from living under an open heaven, then it is no wonder I am fearful and depressed.

A great note of joy and victory is sounded in the book of Philippians—a book, incidentally, written from prison. Here Paul says:

Don't worry about anything; instead, pray about everything; tell God your needs and don't forget to thank him for his answers. If you do this you will experience God's peace, which is far more wonderful than the human mind can understand. His peace will keep your thoughts and your hearts quiet and at rest as you trust in Christ Jesus.

Philippians 4:6–7 TLB

It is God's intention that we live as children of the light. He wants us to be strong, free, peaceful, and happy. This was the secret Nehemiah learned when he was tempted to come down from the wall he was building around the city of Jerusalem. On every side there were worries and fears, but he grasped God's truth and sang, "The joy of the Lord is my strength" (see Nehemiah 8:10).

Now I have a very practical tip for you. Take good notice of all the blessings He gives and all those He has given in your past. As the old hymn says, "Count your many blessings, count them one by one, and it will surprise you, what the Lord has done."

Faith came singing into my room,
And other guests took flight.
Grief, anxiety, fear and gloom,
Sped out into the night.

I wondered that such peace could be,
But Faith said gently, "Don't you see,
That they can never live with me?"

Elizabeth Cheney

6

Frustration

Even if we have learned how to deal with anxiety, worry, and fear, the enemy has yet another powerful weapon he uses on us—frustration. Frustration is dangerous because it is so simple to blame it on others, to think there is nothing we can do to overcome the problem. And yet even the most frustrating of circumstances can be turned to good, if we use the opportunities we have.

I find it a great frustration to have a message but have no one to give it to. On one trip to Russia I had such a frustrating time! I wanted to tell everybody, especially the communists, about the Lord Jesus Christ. However, whenever I tried to talk to people on the streets of Moscow, I found they would always be looking over their shoulders. Finally they would rush away, afraid someone would see them talking to the old woman with a Bible. I became so frustrated, anxious, and filled with despair. I was in Russia, but I could find no one who would listen!

One afternoon I met a young woman, and we chatted about ordinary things—the weather, the tulips in Holland, the price of gasoline. I sensed she was hungry to hear more about the Lord, but I knew she was afraid to talk in the park. I invited her to come to my hotel room for a good talk.

"Oh, no," she whispered, glancing every which way. "The tourist hotel rooms here are the most dangerous places to talk. There is a hidden microphone in each room. Every word you speak is put on a tape and played before the officials." She excused herself and moved quickly away from me.

The next morning my companion and I were sitting in our hotel room, totally defeated. We had been in Russia one week and had not been able to speak to a single communist about the Lord Jesus.

Suddenly I spotted something on the floor, just under the edge of the bed. It was a pattern of tiny holes, like those in the top of a pepper shaker. Suddenly I had a tremendous inspiration. "Thank You, Lord," I said to myself. "That surely must be the place where the microphone is hidden." Reaching for my Bible, I bent low over the holes in the floor and began to speak in a deliberate voice.

"You who listen have many problems, just like every other human being. Two of these problems are common to all men—sin and death. I have here in my hand a book. It almost bursts with good news. In this book—it is called a Bible—you can read everything you need to know about the answers to these problems. The answer is found in the life of a man, the Son of God, Jesus Christ. He died on the cross for the sins of the whole world, and for your sins also. He carried the punishment you and I deserve. But not only did He die for us, He rose from the dead and is alive today. Yes, He is even willing to live in you through His Holy Spirit. If you will accept Him, He will give you the power to overcome death also and live forever with God in heaven."

For almost five minutes I preached into the hidden microphone, knowing that my sermon was not only being heard, but was being recorded on a tape recorder and passed on to superiors. What a joy! I finished my sermon by saying, "Jesus said once, 'Come unto me, all you who labor and are heavy laden, and I will give you rest.' Since all men in Russian know the meaning of labor, then it means that Jesus must love Russians in a special way. When He says 'all,' He is talking to all who listen to this tape."

From that day on, I gave the microphone a little sermon every morning, bringing a simple gospel message and hope to my unseen hearers.

After leaving Moscow, we traveled to Leningrad, where once again I discovered the pepper-shaker holes in the floor. That night I gave a five-minute sermon to my hidden listeners. The next morning, two serious men came in and took a seat next to ours at breakfast. From their appearance and the way they dressed, I was sure they were members of the secret police.

For a moment I was disturbed and frustrated. Then I saw what God was doing. My microphone sermon had brought results! Instead of being worried, I should rejoice. This was simply another opportunity to present the gospel.

I asked my companion, in English, "Do you know that you can become a child of God?"

She immediately grasped what I was doing and began to play her role. "I can never be a child of God," she said, shaking her head. "I am not good enough."

"Ah ha," I answered. "That is exactly what I expected you to say! But you see, only sinners are eligible." As we talked I kept noticing the two men at the next table. They tried to pretend they were not interested. One man had a newspaper in front of his face. But I could see they were leaning in our direction, trying to hear every word.

We continued our conversation, speaking as loudly as we could without making it obvious. We stayed at it until we were satisfied these men could never say they had not heard the gospel. We even repeated the whole conversation in German, in case they couldn't understand my English!

Do you think I was playing a silly game, talking into hidden microphones and giving my testimony at breakfast? It was no game at all! After one whole week of frustration, I was at last giving my message to the communists. Not in the way I would have preferred, it is true. But who can say that those few men who heard me were not important to the Lord? Even when we are denied a big opportunity, we must make the best of all the little ones that come our way.

I remember a story about a little boy and his sister. They were trying to climb a steep mountain. The little girl began to complain, "Why did God put all these rocks here?"

Her brother reached back and patted her on the shoulder. "These are really stepping stones," he said. "God put them here to help us reach the top."

Many people are worried and frustrated because they never have the opportunity to do what they want to do. I have found the seeming obstacles are really opportunities within themselves. If we do what our hand finds to do, then God will open up broader places of service.

Many years ago I heard of an old Dutchman and his young son. They had to walk home at night across the *polders*, the dried sea bottom where the water had been pumped out and held back by dikes. The little boy was afraid, for he knew there were still deep pockets of water and many patches of quicksand on the polders. All they had to give them light on the walk was a small kerosene lantern.

"Please, Father," the boy begged, "don't make me walk out there. It is so dark, and the lamp only gives light enough for one step at a time."

The father took his son's hand in his own. "That's right, but one step at a time is all the light we need. And if we walk in the light we have, we have enough light for the next step. However, if we stand still, waiting for enough light to see the entire way home, then even the light we have will burn out, and we will be left in the dark."

And so they made their way home safely, one step at a time, walking in the light. Every obstacle, every frustration can become an opportunity if we trust God and walk in the light we have.

7

Don't Burden Yourself

L et him have all your worries and cares, for he is
always thinking about you and watching everything
that concerns you" (1 Peter 5:7 TLB).

Many years ago, shortly after World War II had
come to a close, I was invited to speak in a Japanese
church in Tokyo. The nation was still reeling from the
impact of the war. All that the Japanese people had
believed in had been snatched away, and two of their
greatest cities had been destroyed by the atomic bomb.
If ever a people had reason to worry, it was the Japanese.

Because of the language barrier, it seemed practical
for me to give them an object lesson. "Do you know the
feeling," I began, "when your heart is like a suitcase with
a heavy load?"

The sad-faced people in the little church all nodded.
They knew the feeling.

I picked up my suitcase and put it on the table. It was
very heavy. I told them how weary I was from tramping all
over the world, carrying that suitcase filled with heavy
objects.

"My heart was like that until just last week, when I
read a glorious verse in the Bible. It says, 'Cast all your
anxieties on him, for he cares about you.' I did that. I

50

brought all my burdens to the Lord—all my cares—and I cast them upon Him." I opened my suitcase and spread it out on the table to demonstrate. "Lord," I continued, "here are my coworkers. They are so tired." I reached down and took two items out of the suitcase and laid them on the table.

"And here is my trip, Lord—the one I have to make next week to the town where I don't know a single person. You know how worried I am about that, and how afraid I get when I think about it. I cast this care on You, too, Lord." I took a big package out of the suitcase and laid it on the table next to the two smaller packages.

"Here are my friends at home, Lord. They wrote about a car accident. Will you please heal them?" I took out one more object and placed it on the table.

"And here is that boy who refused to give his life to Jesus. Dear Lord, You know how much I have worried about him." I placed a heavy piece on the table.

"This is my unbelief. Almost always when our hearts are heavy, it is because we have an unconfessed sin. Forgive me, Lord, and cleanse me with Your blood. Holy Spirit, give me faith and trust."

I took object after object out of the suitcase, mentioning each one as a particular burden or worry. "This is my pride. This is my self-seeking. . . ." In the end, the suitcase was empty, and I said, "Amen!" I closed the empty suitcase and pretended to walk out of the room, swinging my light bag as though it were made of paper.

The people immediately got my point, and the light of understanding broke on their faces. I could tell by their smiles and polite bows when I was finished that the Holy Spirit had spoken truth to them.

After the meeting I quickly threw all the items back

into the suitcase and dashed off with my host, to go to the home of the wonderful Japanese Christians who entertained me until it was time to fly on to Hong Kong.

Many years passed, and then I found myself in Berlin, at an international congress on evangelism. After one of the morning seminars, a distinguished-looking Japanese evangelist approached me. "Corrie ten Boom," he said with a broad smile, "every time I hear your name, I think of your trouble suitcase."

"Oh," I said, flattered, "I am so glad you remembered what I said that night."

"It was not what you said that I remember," he smiled courteously, "it is what you did."

"You remember me taking all those objects out of my suitcase and laying them on the table as an illustration of how to pray?"

"No, that is not what I remember most," he said. "What I remember most is that after your talk, you took all the objects, put them back in your suitcase, and walked out of the hall just as burdened as when you came in."

Oh, what a vivid object lesson! That afternoon, back in my hotel room, I began to take a good look at myself. Was I guilty of doing that in my life? How easy it is to unpack my trouble suitcase each morning and cast all my cares on the Father, because He cares for me. But then, as the day goes on, I keep coming back and picking up first this care and then that one, slipping them back into my suitcase. By the end of the day, I am just as burdened as I was at the beginning, and far more exhausted, for I have had to keep slipping back to pick up the cares originally given to my Father.

What about you? Did you unpack your trouble suitcase this morning? Good! But what did you do afterwards? Is your heart still as burdened and heavy as it was before you prayed? Did you repack your suitcase as soon as you emptied it? If so, perhaps you need to return to the Lord, casting all your cares upon Him—for He cares for you. Tell it to Him. The Holy Spirit will teach you how to pray and leave your burdens with the Lord.

Live One Day at a Time

When Jesus told His disciples, "Therefore do not be anxious about tomorrow, for tomorrow will be anxious for itself," He was saying, "Don't try to carry today's burden *and* tomorrow's burden at the same time."

One evening a man stepped into the kitchen to help his wife with the dishes. As he was working, he thought, "If that poor woman could just look ahead and see the dishes that remain to be washed in the future, towering like a mountain ahead of her, she would give up right now!" Then he laughed. "But she only has to wash tonight's dishes, and she can handle that."

As you may know, I grew up in a clock shop. My father was a watchmaker, and I was the first woman in Holland to be licensed as a watchmaker. Our home, the Beje, was filled with the sound of ticking clocks. I still remember the old Dutch parable about the clock that had a nervous breakdown.

The little clock had just been finished by the maker, who put it on a shelf in the storeroom. Two older clocks were busy ticking away the noisy seconds next to the young clock.

"Well," said one of the clocks to the newcomer, "so you have started out in life. I am sorry for you. If you'll just think ahead and see how many ticks it takes to tick through one year, you will never make it. It would have been better had the maker never wound you up and set your pendulum swinging."

"Dear me," said the new clock. "I never thought about how many ticks I have to tick in a year."

"Well, you'd better think about it," the old clock said.

So the new clock began to count up the ticks. "Each second requires two ticks, which means 120 ticks per minute," he calculated. "That's 7,200 ticks per hour; 172,800 ticks per day; 1,209,600 ticks per week for fifty-two weeks, which makes a total of 62,899,200 ticks per year. Horrors!" The clock immediately had a nervous breakdown and stopped ticking.

The clock on the other side, who had kept silent during the conversation, now spoke up. "You silly thing! Why do you listen to such words? That old grandfather clock has been unhappy for years. Nobody will buy him, and he just sits around the shop gathering dust. Since he is so unhappy, he tries to make everyone else unhappy, too."

"But," the new clock gasped, "he's right. I've got to tick almost sixty-three million ticks in a year. And they told me I might have to stay on the job for more than one hundred years. Do you know how many ticks that is? That's six billion, two hundred million ticks. I'll never make it!"

"How many ticks do you have to tick at a time?" the wise old clock asked.

"Why only one, I guess," the new clock answered.

"There, now. That's not so hard, is it? Try it along with me. Tick, tock, tick, tock. See how easy it is? Just one tick at a time."

A light of understanding formed on the face of the clock, and he said, "I believe I can do it. Here I go." He began ticking again.

"One more thing," the wise old clock said. "Don't ever think about the next tick until you have your last tick ticked."

I understand that was seventy-five years ago, and the clock is still ticking perfectly, one tick at a time.

No man sinks under the burden of the day. It is only when yesterday's guilt is added to tomorrow's anxiety that our legs buckle and our backs break. It is delightfully easy to live one day at a time!

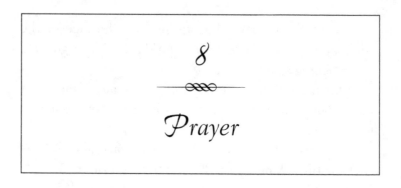

8

Prayer

Sometimes we underestimate the value of our prayers. In the Book of Revelation, we read how precious they are in God's eyes. They are so precious that they are all preserved there.

"Then another angel with a golden censer came and stood at the altar; and a great quantity of incense was given to him to mix with the prayers of God's people, to offer upon the golden altar before the throne. And the perfume of the incense mixed with prayers ascended up to God from the altar where the angel had poured them out" (Revelation 8:3–4 TLB).

When I read this text, I understand a little bit of the great value that our prayers have in the eyes of the heavenly Father. Look back on the prayers you have prayed for that person you are worrying about. Not one of those prayers is lost. They are kept in heaven. What a comfort. What an encouragement!

When Do God's Answers Come?

The Bible says that by prayer and supplication with thanksgiving we should let our requests be made known unto God. Have you ever been discouraged about your praying? Does it seem your prayers are never answered? Much of our anxiety comes as we worry about others. This isn't helped, it seems, if we pray for others and then do not see our prayers answered. However, let me tell you a few stories that I think will give you encouragement to go on, despite seeming failure.

Not very long ago, I had a wonderful experience in my home country of Holland. I was invited to appear on national television to bring the Easter message. More than six million people heard my message, I was told. But the most wonderful result was hearing from some people I had not heard from in years—people I had prayed for many years ago.

One man wrote to me and said, "Twenty-five years ago I came out of a concentration camp, into the house you opened for ex-prisoners. You brought me the gospel. I thought I was not ready for it, but you told me you were going to keep on praying, anyway. Last night I saw you on TV, and now I can say with all my heart, 'I have accepted the Lord.'" It took twenty-five years, but God answered my prayer for that man's salvation!

Another man telephoned. "Forty-five years ago, you told me exactly the same thing you said tonight on TV— that Jesus was the Son of God and is still alive. I always refused to accept Jesus as my personal Savior. Now I am ready to say yes to Him. May I come to see you?"

Of course I replied, "Please come."

We talked and prayed together. "Now," I said, "ask Jesus to come into your heart."

He prayed, "Jesus, I cannot open my heart. Please, won't You force the door?" And Jesus did a miracle in the life of that man—an answer to my prayer after forty-five years.

When I was fifteen years of age, I spent some time at a secular domestic-science school. Most of the teachers and students did not want me to talk about the Lord. Therefore I spent time praying for them. Following the TV broadcast, I received a letter saying, "Sixty years ago we were together at the domestic-science school. I suddenly remembered that you often talked about the Lord Jesus when we were together. I saw and heard you on TV. I just want to write and tell you that I am a follower of Jesus Christ." Another answer to prayer—sixty years after.

But the most amazing answer came the week after the TV broadcast. When I was five years old, I accepted the Lord Jesus as my Savior. After that I developed a burden for the people in my town. We lived in Haarlem, quite near the Smedestraat. In this street there were many pubs. Because of the pubs, I often saw many drunken people, some of whom were dragged into the police station on the same street. I wanted so badly to do something to help, but what can a little girl do in such a sad situation? All I could do was pray—and I did a lot of that.

Mother told me later that for a long time every prayer of mine ended with the words, "Lord Jesus, please save those people in the Smedestraat. And save the policemen, too."

Following my TV appearance, I received a letter. "My husband said that it was so nice to hear that you lived in Haarlem. He lived for seventeen years in the Smedestraat, and he worked in the police station in that street. After I heard you on TV, I knew that you would be interested to know that we now know the Lord personally." It took over seventy years for me to hear that my prayer was answered!

Why do I tell you this? To let you know that no matter

how discouraged you may be over your prayers, God never lets you down.

Pray Alone and Together

Prayer is the sturdy answer to worry. I urge you to find a place where you can be alone with the Lord. Let it be your own little private prayer chapel.

I understand that Susanna Wesley, mother of Charles Wesley, had her own little private prayer closet. When things got bad in the Wesley household—the children screaming, money scarce, the roof leaking—she would reach down and grab the hem of her long skirt. Separating it from the many long petticoats women wore in those days, she would pull the outer skirt up over her head and close herself in. There she would meet the Lord and commune with Him, returning to her hectic world refreshed and revived.

Prayer should be informal and to the point: conversations with God, so to speak. Nice words do not count. Be definite. If you have a nervous tummy, do not ask the Lord to take it away. Rather, confess where you got it and ask Him to shut the door on the source of your worry.

Pray specific prayers. God does not give stones for bread. If you ask for specific things, you will receive specific answers. Most of us receive not because we ask not, or if we do ask, we ask amiss.

Go to God the same way you would go to your father or mother. Tell Him about your worries. Tell Him you are a sinner because you are anxious and nervous. Be definite. Prayer opens doors to the power that relieves us from anxiety, for God's power is demonstrated in our weakness.

Remember, prayer is not one-way traffic. If it were, it would be similar to someone coming into your house, asking a question, and then leaving without waiting for an answer. Prayer is both asking and receiving, speaking and listening. Yes, that takes time. But you can learn how to converse with God secretly.

But there is more. Not only do we find help for our anxiety by praying alone, but also when we pray with others and have others pray for us. Jesus says He enjoys joining a small group of even two or three who are praying in His name. "I will be right there among them" (Matthew 18:20 TLB). What a marvelous promise! But how many take advantage of it? The best place for group prayer is in the family. Are you a mother? Call the children and ask them to pray with you. Tell them you are anxious and worried, and ask them to join you in prayer.

The devil smiles when we make plans. He laughs when we get too busy. But he trembles when we pray—especially when we pray together. Remember, though, that it is God who answers, and He always answers in a way that He knows is best for everybody.

9

God's Answers to Prayer

His love has no limit, His grace has no measure.
   His power no boundary known unto men;
For out of His infinite riches in Jesus,
   He giveth and giveth and giveth again.

Annie Johnson Flint

I know many people who trust the Lord for their eternal safety, but they have no faith for the cares of every day. They would find it easy to die, for they know God has promised them a mansion in heaven. In fact, some of them would like to die, just to escape this world. They have no faith for today—just for tomorrow. They do not see that their daily problems are the material from which God builds His miracles.

Once, when I was a little girl, I remember coming to my father with a broken doll. He was busy in the watch shop repairing clocks and watches, but he stopped what he was doing and took special pains to fix my ragged old doll's broken arm. Why did he take this so seriously? Because he saw the doll through the eyes of his little girl. Your heavenly Father loves you. He sees your problems through your eyes. He loves us all and understands our problems. He cares.

When I was in the German concentration camp at Ravensbrück, one bitter winter morning I woke up with a bad cold. My nose was running. Back in Holland I would have been able to adjust to a cold, because I would have a tissue or a hankie to blow my nose. But in the concentration camp, and without a hankie, I felt I could not stand it.

"Well, why don't you pray for a hankie?" Betsie asked.

I started to laugh. There we were, with the world falling apart around us. We were locked in a camp where thousands of people were being executed each week, being beaten to death, or put through unbearable suffering—and Betsie suggests I pray for a hankie! If I were to pray for anything, it would be for something big, not something little, like that.

But before I could object, Betsie began to pray. "Father, in the name of Jesus I now pray for a hankie for Corrie, because she has a bad cold."

I shook my head and walked away. Very shortly after, I was standing by the window when I heard someone call my name. I looked and spotted a friend of mine, another prisoner, who worked in the hospital.

"Here you are," she said in a matter-of-fact tone. "Take it. I bring you a little present."

I opened the little parcel, and inside was a handkerchief! I could hardly believe my eyes. "How did you know? Did Betsie tell you? Did you know I had a cold?"

She shrugged. "I know nothing. I was busy sewing handkerchiefs out of an old piece of sheet, and there was a voice in my heart saying, 'Take a hankie to Corrie ten Boom.' So there is your gift. From God."

That pocket handkerchief, made from an old piece of sheet, was a message from heaven for me. It told me that there is a heavenly Father who hears, even if one of His children on this planet prays for a tiny little thing like a hankie. Not only does He hear, but He speaks to another of His children and says, "Bring a hankie to Corrie ten Boom."

Why should I worry, when I can pray? We are God's children—His own children. Here is an old and well-known story that taught me a deep lesson.

A boy made a little ship. It was a work of art, and he had put many weeks of work into its construction. When it was ready, he took it to the river, and it could really float. He held the rope tightly in his hand, but suddenly a strong wind swept the boat away with such force that the rope broke. The river was deep and wild, and the boy knew that he had lost his ship.

After a few weeks, to his great joy, he saw his ship in the show window of a shop. He went to the shopkeeper and told him that the ship belonged to him, that he had made it. But the man said, "Only the person who gives me the price I am asking for it will have the ship."

The boy went home crying and told his father, who advised him, "I think you must try to make some money and buy the ship."

The boy worked all his spare time until he had enough money and bought his toy from the man. With his ship in his hand, he came home and said, "It's twice mine! I made it, and I bought it."

Can we trust the Lord Jesus, who made us and bought us?

We surely can. We are twice His!

A minister in Russia gave me another good illustration. Many people lived in a large apartment house. All the junk was taken to the basement and it was over full.

In a corner stood a harp that was broken, and nobody was able to repair it.

Once a tramp asked if he could spend the night in the house. "There is such a severe snowstorm. May I stay here?"

"We have no room for you, but you could sleep in the basement." They emptied a corner and put some straw on the floor.

After some hours, the owner of the harp suddenly heard music in the basement. She ran downstairs and saw the tramp playing the harp.

"How did you repair my harp? I could not find anybody who was able to do it."

The tramp answered, "When I was young I made this harp, and when you make something, you can repair it."

Who made you? Do you think He can repair you?

The No Answer

When Betsie and I were in Ravensbrück, she became very ill. I took her to the prison hospital and she asked me, "Corrie, please pray with me. Ask the Lord Jesus to heal me. He has said, 'If you shall lay hands upon the sick they shall be healed.' Please do that for me."

I prayed and laid hands on her, and both Betsie and I trusted the Lord for healing. The next morning, I ran from the barracks and looked through the window of the hospital and found Betsie's bed was empty. I ran from window to window, until I finally saw her body. They were getting ready to take it to the crematorium. It was the darkest moment of my life.

Then, just a few days later, I was summoned to the prison office. For some reason, I was being released from prison. Surely it was a clerical error, but whatever the cause, I was free to go. It was a miracle of God.

When I came to the office, I discovered nobody there knew that Betsie was dead. So I asked, "Is my sister also free?"

"No. She stays here until the end of the war."

"Can I stay with her?"

The official became furious and shouted at me. "Disappear! Get out of here!"

Suddenly I saw God's side of what had happened. Suppose Betsie had gotten better and I had to leave her behind? I would have been forced to return to Holland and leave her alone in that horrible camp. I could not have stood it. But she had been released from the concentration camp and was now enjoying all the glory of heaven. I walked out of the camp that day praising and thanking the Lord for that unanswered prayer. Yet it really wasn't unanswered. It was answered in God's way, not mine.

So often we pray and then fret anxiously, waiting for God to hurry up and do something. All the while God is waiting for us to calm down, so He can do something through us.

There is a vast difference between prayer in faith and faith in prayer. Faith in prayer is very common. Prayer in faith is so uncommon that our Lord questions if He will find any of it on earth when He comes back. Prayer in faith is a commanded duty; it is always reverently making known our requests unto God in full confidence that, if we ask anything according to His will, He hears us; and that according to our faith an answer to our prayers will be granted us.

Praying in faith comes from an abiding faith in the

Person prayed to—the confidence is in Him. It is based on a knowledge of who He is and on a trusted conviction that He is worthy to be trusted. Praying in faith is the act of a simple-hearted child of God. Can we teach ourselves to pray in faith? We can indeed train ourselves, but the joyful experience is that it is the Spirit of God who does the job. So give room in your heart for the Holy Spirit.

10

Trust

"You should therefore be most careful, my brothers, that there should not be in any of you that wickedness of heart which refuses to trust, and deserts the cause of the living God" (Hebrews 3:12 PHILLIPS). We continue to share in all that Christ has for us so long as we steadily maintain, until the end, the trust with which we began. God's love for us never changes—of this we must be confident.

We sin, and our sin comes between our souls and God, as a dark cloud comes between the sun and the earth, and our communion with Him is broken. We are unable to live in the enjoyment of God's love for us when sin stands in our way. Our temptation to sin by worrying comes from the evil one, but we must remember that he can only come through an open door. Calling on Jesus' name sends him back, along with any of his brood, because they hate and fear the name of their Conqueror. They get away from the sound of that name as fast as they can.

Our fearless testimony makes the power of the blood of Jesus effective. There is great need for overcomers in this world, and our Lord earnestly calls for men to follow in His steps and in His strength. He won the decisive victory over our enemies, but everyone must make that victory his own on the battlefield of his own life. In Jesus' great name, we can. By His grace, we will.

Our worry is often due to physical causes. Overwork always makes a sensitive spirit worry and hurry, which in turn overworks our nerves, until we see things in a distorted manner. It is a vicious circle, because worry usually makes us keep working harder, until we finally drop from exhaustion—physical and mental. At that point, we go to God for help, but we have already begun to listen to the devil, so we go to God with a sense of inferiority, which is the devil's message!

Some years ago, I had a very difficult problem and did not see the answer. I talked it over with a good friend. We looked at each other, and on both of our faces there was an expression of defeat. Suddenly my friend stood up. She hit the table with her hand and said, "Do we really think that the enormous power that caused Jesus to come out of the grave is not enough for our problem?" Then I saw the smallness of my faith. Yes, the same Spirit that raised Christ from the dead is willing to work in you.

But if we want to be victorious over our fears through Jesus' victory and strength, we must also be obedient. It was Jesus' obedience that defeated the enemy at every turn, until the climax of Calvary was reached.

Confessed Sins

Once we realize that fear, anxiety, and worry are sins, and then confess these sins to God, what happens? The Bible says, "He has removed our sins as far away from us as the east is from the west" (Psalm 103:12 TLB). "I've blotted out your sins; they are gone like morning mist at noon!

Oh, return to me, for I have paid the price to set you free" (Isaiah 44:22 TLB). "But if we confess our sins to him, he can be depended on to forgive us and to cleanse us from every wrong" (1 John 1:9 TLB).

Did you ever see a cloud again, after it had disappeared? No, the cloud that appears afterward is a different one. We do not honor God by asking forgiveness a second time for the same sin. Say, "God has beaten this thing. He has forgiven this sin and forgotten it. I can do the same in His strength." Remember that the victory has been won. Claim that victory as your own, and it will be your own in fact. There is far more victory within your reach than you have realized. Reach out your hand and take as your very own what has been done for you. Reckon yourself dead to the sin of worry.

Say with Paul, "I can do everything God asks me to with the help of Christ who gives me the strength and power" (Philippians 4:13 TLB). Commit the past to God, and don't be enchained with it again.

As He cleanses our cups, He fills them to overflowing with His Holy Spirit. We must remember that our cups can be kept clean. Everything that the light of God shows as sin, we can confess and carry to the fountain of water of life, and it is gone, both from God's sight and from our hearts.

A little girl broke a beautiful antique cup. Crying, she brought it to her mother. The mother saw that the little one was sorry, and said, "I forgive you. Throw the pieces in the garbage can."

The next day, the little girl saw the pieces in the garbage can. She took them and brought them to her mother again. "I am so sorry, Mother, that I broke your cup yesterday," she cried.

The mother replied, "Leave that in the garbage can, where it belongs. Remember my forgiveness." A confessed sin is dead. Give it a burial.

"Hallelujah!"

Handel's chorus was resounding through the evening air. "Hallelujah! And He shall reign for ever and ever."

I had never heard it sung so perfectly and in such beautiful surroundings.

We were in Japan. The moon and stars were as clear as they can only be in that country. Far away we even saw the white peaks of Mount Fuji.

"Hallelujah! The Lord God omnipotent reigneth."

I had never heard it sung a capella, without musical accompaniment. It was as if angels were singing.

I knew the girls. They were the students for whom I had been holding a daily Bible study for the last two weeks, and they were going to the same hall as I, where I was expected to answer questions.

That evening I had to listen most to their worry about sins. I prayed that the Lord would give me a clear answer for them. They were Christian girls, but what a lack of joy they had about the finished work of Jesus at the cross. I asked them a question. "When you rehearsed the 'Hallelujah Chorus,' did you make mistakes?"

The girls giggled.

"Many."

"But when you were singing outside in that Japanese moonlit evening, you did not think of those mistakes, otherwise you might have repeated them. Girls, never wait to confess your sins. The devil accuses us night and day. I will tell you something. Sunday morning I spoke in your church."

"Yes, we remember it. You gave us much, but it was so short."

"I thought the same, and your pastor had promised me a long time. I asked him, 'Because I can speak only once in your church, give me as long as possible. Make your preliminaries short.' He promised me, but did not do it. We started the service at ten o'clock, and at eleven o'clock he was still busy with the *Book of Common Prayer*. That moment the Holy Spirit showed me that I was very impatient. I knew that that was a sin, and at 11 o'clock I brought it to the Lord and asked forgiveness. When we confess our sins, He is faithful and just to forgive us and to cleanse us with His blood. Suddenly I saw that the words of the *Book of Common Prayer* were not just preliminaries, but truths that the Lord uses for His honor.

"Why did I tell you that it was eleven o'clock? Because the devil accuses us before God and our own hearts. It is possible that he said to God at 11:05, 'Do You see Corrie ten Boom in Your church and how impatient she is?' I believe that God answered him, 'I already know it. Five minutes ago Corrie told me. It is forgiven and cleansed.'

"Girls, be sure that you are always five minutes earlier than the accuser. Then you lose your worry about your sins. The reason Jesus came to earth was to save sinners. He died for you, so that you could be forgiven, and He lives for you and in you by His Holy Spirit, to make you overcomers. When you worry about your sins it is because you know them through the accuser who has told you, 'That sin is typically you. That is your nature, and you will remain like that your whole life. There is no hope for you.'

"The devil, the accuser, is a liar. When the Holy Spirit convicts you of sin, it is always in the floodlight of the finished work of Jesus at the cross. He tells you: 'Exactly for these sins Jesus died. Confess and be cleansed.'

"Do you remember what I taught you this week—what the Bible says about repented sins? 'As far as the east is from the west, so far does he remove our transgressions from us' [see Psalm 103]. He throws them into the depths of the sea, forgiven and forgotten, and to warn the accuser, He puts a sign saying 'No Fishing Allowed.' Girls, instead of worrying about your sins, sing again, 'Hallelujah! King of kings and Lord of lords.'"

It sounded even more beautiful than when I heard it outside, but this time I saw the happy faces, some still wet with tears.

The Word of God

God's promises were never meant to be thrown aside as waste paper. He intended that they should be used. God's gold is not miser's money, but is minted to be traded with. Nothing pleases our Lord better than to see His promises put into circulation; He loves to see His children bring them up to Him, and say, "Lord do as You have said."

Charles H. Spurgeon

We deny the work of Jesus Christ and stand powerless before the enemy if we doubt the integrity of the Word of God. The bank account of the Bible is not frozen.

Someone told me, "In the Bible there are seventeen thousand promises." I don't know if that is true, but even if there were only seventeen, the quality is so great that the quantity is not too important.

> He has given you the whole world to use, and life and even death are your servants. He has given you all of the present and all of the future. All are yours, and you belong to Christ, and Christ is God's.
>
> *1 Corinthians 3:22–23* TLB

When you check your inventory of blessings from God, it shows you have received good measure, pressed down and running over. Do not say, "I am too great a sinner to appropriate God's promises. Perhaps good Christians may do that, but not I." God always hears a prayer of faith. Put all your needs on the table and then say thank you.

Once a factory owner had a very expensive, complicated machine that he needed for his work. It broke down, and there was nobody who could repair it. The owner sent a telegram to the machine factory: "Send an expert." The very next day, an unimpressive man arrived at the airport. The owner sent another telegram to protest that the man they had sent was unsatisfactory. He wore old clothing, he seemed very uneducated—the owner was not at all happy with him. The answer that came back from the machine factory was, "That man is the designer of your machine."

Don't you think our own Creator can find the answers to our problems? Jesus is able to untangle all the snarls in your soul, to banish all complexes, and to transform even your fixed habit patterns. All you must do is trust Him.

11

Surrender

Jesus told him, 'If you want to be perfect, go and sell everything you have and give the money to the poor, and you will have treasure in heaven; and come, follow me.' But when the young man heard this, he went away sadly, for he was very rich" (Matthew 19:21–22 TLB). That rich young ruler gladly kept all the commandments, and he searched out even more ways to serve his God. But when Jesus told him he would have to give up everything he treasured in his life, the young man simply could not do it.

J. H. Jowett comments on this:

He hallowed the inch, but not the mile. He would go part of the way, but not to the end. And the peril is upon us all. We give ourselves to the Lord, but we reserve some liberties. We offer Him our home, but we mark some rooms "Private." And that word, "Private," denying the Lord admission, crucifies Him afresh.

My being a tramp for the Lord, going over the whole world, was real training for me in surrender and trust. I learned that the safest place in the world is in the center of the will of God. This is always true, even sometimes when it seems as if following God's will is physically dangerous.

Shortly after the war, I was alone in America. It was Saturday morning in Chicago. I paid the taxi driver and stepped into the YWCA. The lady in the office did not look very happy to see me.

"The office is almost closed, lady," she said.

"Have you a room for me?" I asked.

"No. Come back on Monday."

"Will you telephone the nearest police station, then, and ask them if I can sleep in a cell tonight?"

She looked very surprised. "Why?"

"Well, I come from Holland, and in Holland no woman has to stay in the street during the night. There is always room in a police station, in a cell, and I am sure that in America it will be the same. I would not think of remaining on the street all night in a town like Chicago."

She left the office for a minute, then came back and said, "We have found a room for you."

That was exactly what I had hoped would happen, and I went to my room. It was not the most beautiful room. It was very high up in the building and very small, but much more luxurious than the cell I was living in a year before, in the prison camp.

I did not go out on Sunday. It was raining, and I had discovered that when it rains in America, it pours. I needed some time for rest and for talking with the Lord. As a matter of fact, my first experience in Chicago had scared me. I did not know anyone there, and it was such a big, strange city to face alone.

That Sunday in my room, I had a good talk with the Lord. I confessed my fears to Him and surrendered the whole trip through America to His will. Two weeks after, the Lord blessed my ministry in America in a way that must have made the angels rejoice. The Lord did much good work through the many talks in all the little churches. God opened the doors and the hearts of Chicago for me, and Moody Bible Institute gave me such a welcome that I have never since felt alone in Chicago.

My Lord knows the way through the wilderness—all I have to do is follow and to put my hand into His hand. He holds me.

There is only one force more powerful than fear, and that is faith. Does your need seem big to you? Then make sure that God knows how big it looks to your eyes, and He will treat it as such. He will never belittle it, however trivial. He will not laugh at it, or at us. He never forgets how large our problems look to us.

Does your need seem as big as the throne of grace? Do we not there—and there alone—see it in the right proportion?

We ask, "Do you believe that the Lord is your Shepherd?"

"Yes, but . . ."

That fatal word *but* shows that we do not believe the Lord is our Shepherd. "Yes, I believe it, but I do not have victory over my bad temper, and I am not able to win souls. I worry over things. I do not have peace and joy."

The testimony of victory puts *but* into the right place. "I am passing through a time of great sorrow and trouble, but the Lord is my Shepherd. I have been discouraged about my past accomplishment, but the Lord is my Shepherd."

Set yourself against being disturbed by disturbing things. Say to yourself, "Being upset is useless. It has bad results; it is sinful. It reproaches my Master. I will not be upset."

Amy Carmichael wrote:

He, Who loved you unto death, is speaking to you. Listen, do not be deaf and blind to Him. And as you keep quiet and listen, you will know, deep down in your heart, that you are loved. As the air is around about you, so is His love around about you now. Trust that love to guide your lives. It will never, never fail. You know how we have watched the great sea washing over the rocks, flooding them till they overflow? That is what the love of God does for us. We have no love in ourselves and our pools would soon be empty if it were not for that glorious inexhaustible sea of love which extends to you and me. Lord, do Thou turn me all into love, and all my love into obedience, and let my obedience be without interruption.

If His will be your will, and His way be your way, then all your insufficiency and ineptitude shall be met by the sufficiency of His grace.

Obey the voice of the Lord Jesus, who says, "Come unto me, all ye that labour and are heavy laden, and I will give you rest" (Matthew 11:28 KJV). Come! Like a mother says to a fearful child, "Come." Nothing else is necessary. When you come to Him, He does the job.

Jesus says, "Behold, I stand at the door, and knock: if any man hear my voice, and open the door, I will come in" (Revelation 3:20 KJV).

"But as many as received him, to them gave he power to become the sons of God" (John 1:12 KJV). That means to become a member of the very family of God, and

"Except a man be born again, he cannot see the kingdom of God" (John 3:3 KJV). We cannot expect peace or rest until we personally find it in Jesus Christ. When we do, we can say, "For I know whom I have believed, and am persuaded that he is able to keep that which I have committed unto him against that day" (2 Timothy 1:12 KJV).

Know that Christ is the Lord of all: your mind, your spirit, your body. Let Christ's teachings live in your heart, making you rich in true wisdom. Put everything in His hands.

The first time a cowboy heard the story of Jesus riding on an unbroken colt, he exclaimed, "What wonderful hands He must have had!" Consider the hands of Christ: artist's hands that created all the beauty of this world; love-pierced hands of the kindest Friend that man ever had; hands that are aching to take our own and guide us in ways that are good for us; skillful hands, worthy of our trust and love.

Let us let Him clasp our hands a little tighter, and trust Him a little more than ever before—that our paths may be straighter and gladder than in the past. Let us make more time for prayer, so that we increase the pressure of that hand on ours. Their touch is so light, and the whisper so soft, it is easy to miss them.

A young, discouraged artist fell asleep beside the picture that he was trying to complete. His master quietly entered the room, and, bending over the sleeping pupil, placed on the canvas, with his own skillful hand, the beauty that the painting lacked.

When we, tired and spent, lay down the work done in our own strength, our own great Master will make perfect our picture. He will remove every stain, every blemish, and every failure from our service. He will add the brightest luster to our service, and He will give us the highest honor for our work.

Shall we not surrender to the One who can make us His victorious artists? Paul wrote:

> My brothers, I do not consider myself to have grasped it fully even now. But I do concentrate on this: I leave the past behind and with hands outstretched to what-ever lies ahead I go straight for the goal—my reward the honor of being called by God in Christ.
>
> *Philippians* 3:13–14 PHILLIPS

> Now to him who is able to keep you from falling and to present you before his glory without fault and with unspeakable joy, to the only God, our Savior, be glory and majesty, power and authority.
>
> *Jude 24* PHILLIPS

12

Good News

There are so many people living close to all of us who do not know the Lord Jesus and who need to have His great love explained to them. If we do not do it, who will? The time is short; eternity is so very long. Let us be busy in the Lord's work and ask Him to use us to bring others to Him. "How beautiful are the feet of them that preach the gospel of peace, and bring glad tidings of good things!" (Romans 10:15 KJV).

Once in Switzerland a mother brought me her little daughter who was ten years old. She said, "Can you tell this girl how to become a child of God? She always goes to Sunday school and really knows everything, but I can't tell her what to do to become a child of God."

I took the girl aside and said, "Look, imagine that I wanted to adopt you as my child. Once I had the proper papers I could just say, 'Now you are my child.' But I wouldn't do it that way. I would wait until I saw that you liked me and then I would ask you, 'Do you want to become my child?'

"Then, if you should say, 'Yes, I would like to become your child very much,' I would continue and tell you, 'All right, here are the papers. They have been ready for a long time. I did not use them until now because you had not decided that you loved me and wanted to become my child.'

"The Lord Jesus asks you now, 'Will you become a child of God?' If you say, 'Yes, Lord, I will,' He will tell you, 'All is ready. The preparations were all taken care of at the cross. I have paid the price so that you can become a child of God. We have waited for the decision to come from you.'"

Then I read with her John 1:12: "As many as received him, to them gave he power to become the sons of God, even to them that believe on his name" (KJV).

We knelt down after that and the girl accepted the Lord. I can tell you her happy face was more beautiful than the snow-tops of the Alps on the horizon. Is it really so simple?

In Germany a woman told me that forty-two years ago she had committed a terrible sin and since then she had prayed every day for forgiveness. Poor soul! She did not know, like so many people do not know, that the sin problem has been solved at Calvary's cross.

The moment that you believe, you are registered in heaven as one of those who has rights and privileges that make you a multimillionaire in the spiritual realm. Faith is a problem for those who do not know the Bible and the Lord. God says, "I am watching over my word to perform it" (Jeremiah 1:12 RSV). When the heart has learned to trust Him as He should be trusted—utterly, without reservation—then the Lord throws wide the doors of the treasure house of grace. He bids us to come in with boldness so that we may receive our share of the inheritance of the saints in life.

The Bible is full of overflowing riches and victory. "The God and Father . . . who hath blessed us with all spiritual blessings . . . in Christ" (Ephesians 1:3 KJV) means that the moment we accept Jesus Christ as our Savior and confess Him as our Lord, everything God wrought in Christ belongs to us. It is ours. Often people say, "I hope that I am a child of God," or, "I try to be a Christian." I believe that we are too often failure-conscious. Faith makes us victory-conscious. Faith brings the unreality of hope to the reality of now. Hope is future. Faith is present. Faith is the radar that shows us the reality of Christ's victory. The moment that radar works correctly, we dare to say, "God has made me able to conquer weakness, fear, and inability, and I stand and declare that whosoever believes in Jesus shall not be put to shame."

Jesus was Victor, Jesus is Victor, Jesus will be Victor. Hallelujah!

13

A Child Shall Lead Them

Children can be such joyful additions to our so often serious and stuffy world. They open our eyes to the wonders of creation and make us consider such important questions as, "How do the stars stay in the sky?" and "Why is the grass green instead of red?" Their laughter brightens many lives.

In my years of traveling I was often touched by children because of their honesty and open expressions of emotion. They aren't afraid to admit weakness, yet they will often defend what they know to be right, regardless of the circumstances or possible results.

I remember one story of an East German teacher who told her class that God does not exist. After her lesson, she asked who still believed in God, and a little girl stood up. The teacher made her stay after school and write one hundred times, "I do not believe God exists." The girl could not do that, so she wrote, "I do believe God exists." The teacher was so angry with her that she made her write it correctly one thousand times at home that night. The little girl wrote it one thousand times her way, although she knew she would be punished severely in school the next day. This young child believed in God and was not going to deny Him in spite of the consequences. What an important lesson for all of us to learn!

In addition to being open about their feelings, children have a very special freedom in their communication with their heavenly Father. They aren't held back by the barriers that adults build between themselves and the Lord.

A mother I met told me that she saw her little boy sitting in a corner of the room, saying "A-B-C-D-E-F-G . . ."

"What are you doing?" she asked.

"Mom, you told me I should pray, but I have never prayed in my life and I don't know how. So I gave God the whole alphabet and asked Him to make a good prayer of it."

That boy understood a little bit of what Paul wrote in Romans 8:26—that the Holy Spirit Himself helps us to pray.

Another very important lesson we can learn from children is seen in their relationship with their parents. In my family we knew that we were loved. Our parents had our very best interests in mind; there was never any doubt about that. They were totally trustworthy, and in our home we children always felt secure and protected. Our parents' love for us was an excellent introduction to the relationship we came to share with our heavenly Father. We are His precious children. His love for us is so great that we can't even begin to understand it. In the midst of hurrying about and being concerned with so many details of daily living, we must always remember that God's love can make us conquerors if we receive Him as a child—with an open and trusting heart.

14

The Three Locks

"Let us search and try our ways, and turn again to the Lord" (Lamentations 3:40 KJV). Three times in my life locks were closed behind me and, after a time of imprisonment, opened again.

I learned how it feels to be behind a door that can be opened only from the outside. Those were difficult classes in life's school, but in a difficult class one learns much, especially when there is a good teacher.

My Teacher was the Lord. He made me learn from experience that, for a child of God, a pit can be very deep, but always below us are the everlasting arms of our Lord.

The first lock that closed behind me left me in a cell where I was in solitary confinement for about four months. In my book *Prison Letters* you can read what a miracle of blessing I experienced. The fellowship with the Lord was so precious that I wrote to friends outside, "Please never worry about me; sometimes it may be dark, but the Savior provides His light and how wonderful that is. I am surprised that I can adjust so well to being alone in a prison cell."

My sister Betsie, who was in a different cell, wrote, "This horror has come to us from God's loving hands to purify me."

When the second lock closed behind Betsie and me, we were in Vught concentration camp where I learned another lesson. I wrote from Vught, "We are in God's training school and learning much. We are continually protected by the most extraordinary providence, and we know that we can hold out in spite of the hard life. God knows the way; we are at peace with everything."

The third lock was closed behind us in Ravensbrück, the terrible concentration camp north of Berlin. For Betsie, the lock was opened when the Lord took her to Him.

To enter into Heaven's rest
And yet to serve the Master blest,
From service good, to service best.

For me the door opened to a wide, wide world where I became a tramp for the Lord, going wherever I could tell what I had learned: When the worst happens in the life of a child of God, the best remains and the very best is yet to be.

I have seen many people behind closed doors in the more than sixty countries where I have worked. Some were behind the solid rock of hatred. Many were liberated through claiming Romans 5:5 and by asking forgiveness for their sins.

"Forgiveness is the key that unlocks the door of resentment and the handcuffs of hatred. It is a power that breaks the chains of bitterness and the shackles of selfishness." Whom the Lord makes free, is free indeed— that I saw in the lives of people who were behind the locks of bondage to drugs, alcohol, and smoking.

Self is a tight lock. I saw many decent sinners who were in a kind of spiritual prison because self was on the throne of their hearts and Jesus was on the cross. What a liberation came when Jesus cleansed the heart with His blood. Then He came to the throne, and self went on the cross.

My friends, is there still a closed lock in your life? Jesus is willing to set you free.

"I will all the more gladly boast of my weaknesses, that the power of Christ may rest upon me" (2 Corinthians 12:9 RSV).

15

The Power of Prayer

When I was a little girl I was sure that Jesus was a member of the ten Boom family. It was just as easy to talk to Him as it was to carry on a conversation with my mother and father. Jesus was there. I was closer to the reality and truth of Jesus' presence than the one who makes fellowship with the Lord a problem by reasoning and logical thinking.

Prayer is a joy and a privilege, available to all of God's children. The Lord longs to hear all of our concerns—any concern too small to be turned into a prayer is too small to be made into a burden.

My father prayed because he had a good Friend with whom to share the problems of the day. He prayed because he had a direct connection with his Maker when he had a concern. He prayed because there was so much for which he was thankful.

Prayers should be informal and to the point—conversation with God, so to speak. Remember, prayer is not one-way traffic. If it were, it would be similar to someone coming into your house, asking a question, and then leaving without waiting for an answer. Prayer is both asking and receiving, speaking and listening. Yes, that takes time. But you can learn how to converse with God.

An important thing to remember when praying is that Jesus is our Advocate before the Father. When we begin or end our prayers with "in the name of Jesus," it is just as if Jesus Himself is saying, "Father, this is a prayer from your beloved child, Mary [or John or Carol . . .]." That prayer is sanctified by the name of Jesus. The name that is above every other in heaven or on earth is Jesus, Savior! He is our strength.

"There is salvation in no one else, for there is no other name under heaven given among men by which we must be saved" (Acts 4:12 RSV).

Jesus' example of intercession is one we should follow. The greatest thing one person can do for another is to pray for him. If at this moment you pray for someone, even though he is on the other side of the globe, the Lord Jesus will touch him.

When I am fearful or anxious for myself, I pray for others. I pray for everyone who comes into my thoughts—people with whom I have traveled, those who were in prison with me, my school friends of years ago. My fear soon disappears. Interceding for others releases me.

However, prayer should never be an excuse for inaction. Nehemiah prayed, but he also set guards for protection. He used common sense. As a result, what had not been done in a hundred years' time was finished in fifty-two days.

Sometimes God's answers to our prayers are not as clear to us as was His response to Nehemiah. But we must never doubt that God hears our prayers. Often when we think that God has not answered, He is saying, "Wait." His timing is perfect.

In order to receive answers we need to pray specific prayers. God does not give stones for bread. By asking for specific things, we will receive specific answers. Most of us do not receive because we do not ask (see James 4:2).

Prayer is powerful. The devil smiles when we make plans. He laughs when we get too busy. But he trembles when we pray—especially when we pray together. Remember, though, that it is God who answers, and He always answers in a way that He knows is best for everyone.

When man listens, God speaks.
When man obeys, God acts.
When man prays, God empowers.

16

I Was in Prison, but He Was with Me

Do you ever feel alone? What a question! Of course you do. But I know from my own experience that the worst loneliness is that of solitary confinement.

Years ago I was alone in a cell for four months. One day for the first time a beam of sunlight shone through the window. I jumped up and stood so that the sunshine touched my face. Slowly it moved on and I moved too, just to enjoy that beam as long as possible.

That was one of the moments when I realized my loneliness as never before. I cried to the Lord, and He answered: "Have you forgotten that there is always, under all circumstances, the sunshine of My love? Have I not said: 'Lo, I am with you alway, even unto the end of the world' [Matthew 28:20 KJV]? I am your peace. I can give you joy now also."

I started to sing, first softly, later more loudly:

What a friend we have in Jesus,
All our sins and griefs to bear.
What a privilege to carry
Everything to God in prayer.

I waited a moment, and then I heard from another cell:

O what peace we often forfeit,
O what needless pain we bear,
All because we do not carry
Everything to God in prayer.

It was an answer from a woman who also was in solitary confinement. Her husband had been shot before her eyes, then she had been put in prison. But she, too, knew Jesus as her Friend and Savior. I answered her by singing:

Have we trials and temptations?
Is there trouble anywhere?
We should never be discouraged
Take it to the Lord in prayer!

Can we find a friend so faithful,
Who will all our sorrows share?
Jesus knows our every weakness,
Take it to the Lord in prayer.

A guard banged on the door and shouted, "If you do not stop singing, I will take you to the dark cell."

I stopped singing and threw myself onto my dirty bed. There was peace in my heart. The guard did not know when I sang so softly that only my Savior could hear:

Are we weak and heavy-laden
Cumbered with a load of care?
Precious Savior, still our refuge
Take it to the Lord in prayer.

Do thy friends despise, forsake thee?
Take it to the Lord in prayer!
In His arms He'll take and shield thee,
Thou wilt find a solace there.

Not only in solitary confinement can one feel alone. Often in the company of many others with whom you have no real fellowship you can be lonely. But Jesus is with you also. Have you asked Him to come into your heart? Then you can talk to Him without saying one word aloud. He hears and He loves you. You are very precious in His eyes. Hallelujah, what a Savior!

17

∞

A Higher Wisdom

How we need to have good vision in this time when all is so dark. The Holy Spirit gives us good eyes, that we may see God's plan in the midst of all the chaos of this time.

In 1 Corinthians 1 and 2, Paul talks about the "foolishness" of God and the "wisdom" of the wise. These are two realms we need to recognize. The wisdom of the wise is all we can grasp with our logical thinking, with our brains. The foolishness of God, the greatest wisdom, we can only touch with our faith knowledge. The Holy Spirit teaches us to lift up the wisdom of the wise to the height of the foolishness of God, and then we get the vision.

When people do not know the Lord and are not born into the family of God, they cannot see or understand the kingdom of God, because they have only their logical thinking, the use of their brains. And when you try to bring the foolishness of God under the criticism of the wisdom of the wise, then you may end up with a theology that says, "God is dead."

We live in an age when one of the signs of the end time which Daniel gave is becoming very clear: "knowledge shall increase" (Daniel 12:4 RSV). Some people expect that in the coming ten years the sum total of human knowledge will be doubled.

It is such a great danger when only our logical thinking gives us guidance. It may become a weapon in the hands of the antichrist. I experienced that personally once at a congress of communists in Ravensbrück. I had heard that a reunion of ex-prisoners was to be held, and I had hoped to find friends there with whom I had suffered. Instead, forty thousand communists were present.

I listened to their talks, and such darkness fell upon me that when I returned to West Germany, I felt that I had no message with me. The Lord liberated me totally, and I received a strong message from Him. But there I saw how dangerous it is to be permanently in the atmosphere of the wisdom of the wise without any knowledge of the foolishness of God, which is the highest wisdom.

Earthly wisdom is not something that is wrong in itself. We belong to the Lord one hundred percent, heart and mind. When we have surrendered both to Him, He will show us how to use that wisdom. I remember that when I was a watchmaker with my father, he once said: "My name is on the shop, but really God's name should be there, because I am a watchmaker by the grace of God."

Sometimes when we could not find what was wrong with a watch, we prayed that the Lord would show it to us. And Father and I both had the joyful experience that in our dreams in the night the Lord showed us the fault in a watch. When it happened with me, I went down to the workshop and looked to see if my dream was true. I always found that it was. Yes, there is nothing too great for God's power, nothing too small for His love.

When I worked in Vietnam, a doctor came to me when I had a bad case of enteritis. First he prayed with me and claimed victory over the sickness that tried to keep me away from the important work I had to do there. After that, he gave me some very good medicine. I saw that this man knew both the wisdom of the wise and the foolishness of God.

A space traveler once said: "I was very high up in space, but I never saw God." That man knew only the wisdom of the wise. We who belong to Jesus can find the wisdom of God, which may be foolishness in the eyes of the world, but for us it is a great power to find the way though this dark time we are now experiencing. James tells us where we can find that power: "If any of you lacks wisdom, let him ask God, who gives to all men generously and without reproaching, and it will be given him. But let him ask in faith, with no doubting" (James 1:5–6 RSV).

18

❦

Unfolding God's Love Letter

"All scripture is inspired by God and profitable for teaching, for reproof, for correction, and for training in righteousness, that the man of God may be complete, equipped for every good work" (2 Timothy 3:16–17 RSV). Reading the Bible is the best way to come to know the Lord Jesus, and yet many times it can be difficult. A good Dutch friend gave me some very practical advice on how to study the Word.

"Once the Bible was a closed book to me, but now it has come alive. I am longing to receive more of its treasures. I have been given victory over my sins, and my life has become happier. You may be in the same position I was in. Perhaps you reached out for the Bible when you gave your life to Christ. For a while it was interesting, but then you stopped reading, and now you are discouraged and do not try to read any more.

"Are you longing to know the Bible? I believe I have found a good method for Bible study. The first thing you must do to study the Bible is to realize that the Bible is God's book, His love letter to you. If you know that you are in contact with God through faith in the forgiveness of your sins by Jesus Christ, then the Bible can become a living book for you, full of rich treasures. It is only with this realization that you can truly understand the Bible.

"Next you must ask God for His help and believe that He hears your prayer.

"Now take your Bible and choose a book to study. Let us start with the Gospel of John, chapter 1, verses 1–14.

"Ask yourself, 'What is the most beautiful verse and why is this so?' In John, I believe verse 12 is the most beautiful: 'But as many as received him, to them gave he power to become the sons of God, even to them that believe on his name' [KJV].

"I find this beautiful because there is no other condition which is required to become a child of God than faith.

"Now look through the passage again and consider the question, 'Is there a promise for me in this section?' A young man once said to me after he studied this question, 'I have received a new Bible, for I have found Christ in it.'

"A girl in a Bible study camp once found a wonderful promise in verse 9: He 'lighteth every man.' This made her very happy, she told me with shining eyes, because she knew now that God seeks contact with every person from the beginning of his life.

"Next, examine the passage to see if there is a warning in it. I find in verse 11: 'his own received him not.' This is a warning that we may pass on to others, to all with whom we have an opportunity to speak of Jesus Christ. Not receiving Him means to go into eternity unsaved.

"The last question to ask is, 'Did a prayer come into my heart while I was reading this passage?' I wanted to pray while I was reading verse 4: 'Lord, grant that many may see that light and commit themselves to You.'

"Is Bible study difficult? No. It just requires some

time and prayer. Try to get some friends together, and use this method of Bible study. If you read your Bible, I am sure that you will experience its power in your life."

My friend is right; Bible study is not difficult. Understanding the Bible does not depend upon the wisdom of your mind or mine. We should never use the standards of our own reason when we read the Scriptures.

If only we would accept the Bible in a simple, child-like way, as the Word of God, the Word that teaches us about the foolishness of God which is wiser than the wisdom of men, and the love of God that passes all understanding. How greatly it would change our lives; we would begin to see things in the right perspective. We need never fear to trust in the Word, because the Bible is absolutely reliable.

I will tell you some reasons why I believe that the Bible is inspired. First of all, it says so! "Holy men of God spake as they were moved by the Holy Ghost" (2 Peter 1:21 KJV).

I also look at the effect it has had on all who believe and follow it. How could it have had so much influence without the Holy Spirit? Also, even though some of the books were written more than two thousand years apart, the writers agree.

Against human nature, the authors do not offer any excuse for their own faults or sins. They record the most harrowing scenes that affected them very much, yet they never express one word of emotion. The Holy Spirit wanted the facts recorded and not their feelings about the facts.

How wonderful to have a love letter from God! He took the time to write it; shouldn't we take more time to read it?

19

The Protection
of the Most High

Trust in the LORD with all your heart,
And do not lean on your own understanding.
In all your ways acknowledge Him,
And He will make your paths straight.

Proverbs 3:5–6 NASB

Many people came to know and trust the Lord during World War II. One was an Englishman who was held in a German prison camp for a long period of time.

One day he read Psalm 91:

He who dwells in the shelter of the Most High
Will abide in the shadow of the Almighty.
I will say to the Lord, "My refuge and my fortress,
My God, in whom I trust!"
For you have made the Lord, my refuge,
Even the Most High, your dwelling place.
No evil will befall you,
Nor will any plague come near your tent.

For He will give His angels charge concerning you,
To guard you in all your ways.

Psalm 91:1–2, 9–11 NASB

"Father in heaven," he prayed, "I see all these men dying around me, one after the other. Will I also have to die here? I am still young and I very much want to work in Your kingdom here on earth."

He received this answer: "Rely on what you have just read and go home!"

Trusting in the Lord, he got up and walked into the corridor toward the gate. A guard called out, "Prisoner, where are you going?"

"I am under the protection of the Most High," he replied. The guard came to attention and let him pass, for Adolf Hitler was known as "the Most High."

He came to the gate, where a group of guards stood. They commanded him to stop and asked where he was going.

"I am under the protection of the Most High." All the guards stood at attention as he walked out the gate.

The English officer made his way through the German countryside and eventually reached England, where he told how he had made his escape.

He was the only one to come out of that prison alive.

20

Outside His Boundaries

S tay always within the boundaries where God's love can reach and bless you" (Jude 21 TLB). During the war I had an experience that reminded me how important it is to stay in the center of God's will—the safest place in the world.

After I came home from Ravensbrück, a man I did not know came to see me one day. He showed me a paper and said that a friend of his was in prison and that his life was in danger.

"You know the governor of that prison," he said. "He is a good Hollander and he is on our side. Will you come and introduce me to him, give him this paper, and ask him to release my friend?"

"I don't think I know that governor," I told him, "but I am willing to come with you. Let us pray first, however, that the Lord may protect us."

On bikes without tires we went to the prison and rang the bell. When the guard opened the door, I asked to speak to the governor. As the door closed behind us, I began to feel uncomfortable. When I saw the governor I knew I had never met him before.

"May I talk with you just a moment?" I asked.

He took us down a corridor till we were in the center

of the prison. I gave the paper to him. He looked at it, then said, "Wait a minute. I'll call the Gestapo to see whether or not this request can be granted."

My heart sank. Had my companion mistaken me for someone else?

"No, no, let me just talk with you a moment," I said. But he left.

The governor was gone for perhaps five minutes. While we waited, I recognized the prison smell I knew so well. I heard a man pounding on the door of his cell, crying, "Let me go! I want to get out of here! Open the door!"

This was all too familiar to me; I began to tremble. Could my liberty have been so short? A terrible fear came over me, a fear I had not felt during all the time I was in Ravensbrück.

The governor returned and led us to his office. When he had shut the door, he turned to me and said, "Are you an underground worker? How stupid you are! Look at this paper. There are three very big errors in it."

I knew it was not my fault, but I listened to his reprimand with joy; he was telling me that he was an underground worker and a good Dutchman, so I need not fear anything.

"If I did what you ask," he continued, "I would have to go underground at once with all my helpers. I intend to stay here and help until the last day of the war."

Then he looked at me and sighed. "I will tell you how you can get this young man free."

"Tell this man, please," I said, gesturing toward my companion. While I listened to their voices, the room whirled around me. My heartbeat became normal again only when I was safely out of the prison.

"You looked so scared," my companion said as we were walking out. "I was told you were never afraid. You looked like a ghost."

Yes, I had been afraid. Was I the same Corrie ten Boom who stood in pitch dark in the concentration camp, comforting my friends as they went to their deaths?

I was the same Corrie ten Boom. But in the concentration camp I was in the place where God had called me, and He was my strength. Here I was not in His will, and without Him I was nothing—I was stupid, weak, and helpless.

After this incident my friends forbade me to do any more underground work. I agreed.

On the last day of the war, the prison governor released eighteen prisoners who were to be shot that day. He and all the guards who had helped him escaped in the nick of time.

21

The Fullness of the Spirit

We can expect Jesus' coming very soon, and we must be ready. As the wise virgins had oil in their lamps, so we have to be filled with the Holy Spirit. The wise virgins refused to give half of their oil to the foolish virgins, because they knew that half a portion was not sufficient to reach the house of celebration and to light their lamps during the marriage feast. So we must have our full portion of the Holy Spirit to be ready for Jesus' coming.

What joy it is that He is willing to fill our hearts like a light is ready to fill a room that is open to its brightness. Let us only offer Him a clean house. That is possible when we bring all our unconfessed sins to the Lord and claim 1 John 1:7, the cleansing by the blood of Jesus.

Being filled with the Spirit is not so much a question of striving but of surrendering to Him who will keep you steadfast in the faith to the end, so that when His day comes, you need fear no condemnation (see 1 Corinthians 1:8).

Let us not underestimate the power and work of the Holy Spirit. The Word of God tells us: "Ye must be born again . . . born of the Spirit" (John 3:7–8 KJV). To be "born again" means not only our turning to God, but God's putting His Spirit within us to be the new life in our souls, thus making us children of God.

I have discovered three steps in being born of the Holy Spirit: receive, recognize, and rely.

Receive: In seeking this new life, your part is to turn from sin to God, claim your union with the Savior who died and rose again for you, and ask for and receive the Holy Spirit.

Jesus' part is to put all the past under His blood and to breathe into your heart His Holy Spirit to cause you to know Him as a personal Savior. Therefore ask, and by faith, receive the Holy Spirit, because God, who cannot fail, promises to give to all those who ask. Prove your faith by giving thanks to God and by bearing witness to men of the covenant made with God.

Recognize: Recognize that the Holy Spirit is within you, and obey Him in all things. Remember you have opened your heart to a divine Person, the third Person of the Trinity, who has come to "lead you into all truth." Beware of forgetting your contract with God. God must have first place in your heart and life. Do not wait for "feelings," but expect the Holy Spirit to teach you, convict you of sin, and transform you until you are well-pleasing in His sight.

Rely: Rely upon the Holy Spirit within you to give you victory over every temptation of the devil and make you more than a conqueror. As you read God's Word, ask Him especially to speak some promise to your heart, witnessing that the Holy Spirit has come to you; thus you will be ready to meet the tempter with the Sword of the Spirit. Rely on the Holy Spirit for everything. Long for anything that is God's will for you, and trust Him to work in you.

I tell you, Ask, and it will be given you; seek, and you will find; knock, and it will be opened to you. . . . What father among you, if his son asks for a fish, will instead of a fish give him a serpent . . . ? If you then, who are evil, know how to give good gifts to your children, how much more will your heavenly Father give the Holy Spirit to those who ask him!

Luke 11:9, 11, 13 RSV

22

Trust and Obey

Did you testify to your faith this week? The Lord used you. Did you get discouraged? Perhaps you will not see it here, but in heaven you will see how the Lord has used you. Trust and obey. "Let nothing move you as you busy yourselves in the Lord's work. Be [assured] that nothing you do for him is ever lost or ever wasted" (1 Corinthians 15:58 PHILLIPS).

I remember that when I worked in Russia, there was a time when I did not have many opportunities to witness. But in the hotel were two American people who always tried to sit at our table. How they loved to hear us talk about the Lord Jesus. Later, we lost their address, and so I lost contact with them. What a joy when a year later I received a letter from the lady who told me, "What a lot my husband and I learned through the conversations at the hotel dining room table in Moscow. My husband died last month, and he knew that his sins were forgiven through Jesus Christ. God used you to show us the way."

When you trust and obey, the Lord does the job. Hallelujah!

23

~∞~

The Good Fight

Often I have heard people say, "How good God is. We prayed that it would not rain for our church picnic, and look at this lovely weather!" Yes, God is good when He sends good weather. But God was also good when He allowed my sister Betsie to starve to death before my eyes in the German concentration camp. "For just as the sufferings of Christ are ours in abundance, so also our comfort is abundant through Christ" (2 Corinthians 1:5 NASB).

I remember one occasion when I was very discouraged there. Everything around us was dark, and there was darkness in my heart. I remember telling Betsie that I thought God had forgotten us.

"No, Corrie," said Betsie, "He has not forgotten us. Remember His Word: 'For as the heaven is high above the earth, so great is his mercy toward them that fear him . . .' [Psalm 103:11 KJV]."

The Lord in His love accepts us as we are, and if we are obeying Him, He will work through us, whatever our circumstances.

I was very moved when in Russia I met a woman who was totally dedicated to typing out Christian books on her typewriter. She was paralyzed—only one finger could be moved. She was in bed, and an old typewriter stood in front of her bed on a small table. Yet she had typed out many Christian books. She was very gifted and had read a great number of books. Among many others, she had translated my books and given them to people.

Very often we say that we have no time and strength to work for the Lord. I was ashamed when I saw this woman. Able to move only one finger, she spent many hours a day typing to spread the gospel. The Lord wants to use everybody, if only we will be obedient and are in the center of His will.

Perhaps you think, "I don't have enough faith." Hudson Taylor, the great missionary to China, said, "It is not a great faith that we need, but faith in a great God." Jesus said that even if our faith is as small as a mustard seed, we can move mountains.

When the jailer at Philippi asked Paul and Silas, "What must I do to be saved?" they answered, "Believe on the Lord Jesus Christ, and thou shalt be saved" (Acts 16:30–31 KJV). When you take this step you become a child of God; you are on the Lord's side at the very moment you enter through the door of faith.

This is the great beginning of the fight of faith, and we need the armor of God so that we may stand our ground even when we have come to a standstill. But it is a fight of victory; the Lord throws open wide the door of faith's treasure-house of plenty and bids us enter and take with boldness.

God blesses you. There is an ocean of God's love available through the Holy Spirit (see Romans 5:5). There is plenty for everyone. May God grant you never to doubt that victorious love—whatever the circumstances.

God hath not given us the spirit of fear; but of power, and of love, and of a sound mind.

2 Timothy 1:7 KJV

Share in suffering as a good soldier of Christ Jesus. . . . An athlete is not crowned unless he competes according to the rules.

2 Timothy 2:3, 5 RSV

24

———— ∞∞∞ ————

Everlasting Life

As far astern as one could go on the deck of a freighter, I found a quiet spot where I could be delightfully alone.

I leaned on the rail and gazed at the silver wake left by our boat on the surface of the sea. Dolphins were leaping out of the water. Seven seagulls were circling around the ship. They would follow us faithfully until land was again within sight.

I mused.

What a tiny cockle-shell our vessel is on the immensity of the sea!

What a minute, insignificant, and temporal creature I am! Between my birth and my death I am permitted to live on this earth for some time and after that . . . eternity.

Where am I exactly?

Here I am aboard a tiny ship, and deep, deep under me is the sea, full of the mysterious life of marine animals. Above me is the infinite sky, out of which a tempest might come to wreck this little vessel. Around me is the endless sea, in which so many people have drowned.

From *Amazing Love* by Corrie ten Boom, 111–12. Copyright © 1957.

Where, exactly, am I?

I live in a world where demons rule, where wars are waged, where millions of people are starving, where cities are turned into ruins in many parts of [the world]; where atom bombs are surpassed in destructive power by hydrogen bombs.

Exactly where am I?

I am in a world which God so loved, "that he gave his only begotten Son, that whosoever believeth in him should not perish, but have everlasting life" (John 3:16 KJV).

I am on an earth where soon He shall come, even He who has promised, "Behold, I make all things new" (Revelation 21:5 KJV).

One day the earth, this beautiful earth, "shall be filled with the knowledge of the glory of the LORD, as the waters cover the sea" (Habakkuk 2:14 KJV).

Where am I exactly?

Already, at this moment, I am in Him.

And underneath me are His eternal arms.

"May the God of peace himself sanctify you wholly; and may your spirit and soul and body be kept sound and blameless at the coming of our Lord Jesus Christ" (1 Thessalonians 5:23 RSV).

25

Red Cap 42

Corporate prayer is a mighty weapon. I often experienced this in the concentration camp. It drives demons away. Of the many prayer groups I have known in America, the prayer group of Red Cap 42 was a remarkable one. He was a black man whom I met during my traveling days at his stand in Grand Central Station, New York.

The doors to the tracks were opened only ten minutes before the trains left. The Red Caps had the keys to these doors. Three times a week at noon, Ralston Crosby Young, Red Cap 42, gathered his friends and a few newcomers—people from all walks of society—in front of one of these doors. When all were present, he opened the door and preceded them down the stairs to an empty train at the underground platform. They sat down in a compartment, and Ralston said a short prayer and read a Bible portion. Then he told something about his life and conversion and invited others to say a few words. Some of them told about their difficulties, others of Christ's victories in their lives, and then many prayed in turn, short and powerful prayers.

It was dark in the compartment and on the platform, for the lights were turned on only when the train left.

Here these people were gathered in the heart of New York City, each one with his or her cares and struggles and their longing to serve Christ. Together they sought their strength in prayer. Their meeting time was halfway between their working hours. Perhaps it was nothing special they were discussing, but together these people were close to God for a while.

A little later, travelers flooded onto the platform and each one went to his or her office, school, factory, or wherever the work was waiting. Red Cap 42 took the luggage of an old lady who did not know the way and was looking anxiously around her. She asked him something, and then I heard him answer: "Just pray!"

Say, did you pray today? Did you tell everything to God? He loves you and understands you. There is nothing too great for His power; there is nothing too small for His love. "For I am confident of this very thing, that He who began a good work in you will perfect it until the day of Christ Jesus" (Philippians 1:6 NASB).

26

Christ in You

A millionaire once prayed at every meeting of his church for the fullness of the Holy Spirit. Someone said to him, "Do you know what that means? The Holy Spirit must also come into your pocketbook!"

For four weeks the man would not pray for the fullness of the Holy Spirit. But he finally realized that his money was not making him happy, fulfilled, or at peace. After he asked again to receive the Holy Spirit, the Lord directed the man to give money to do His work; but, of course, the man soon found his life to be even richer because he had allowed the Spirit to take control.

Hudson Taylor said, "God gives the Holy Spirit not to those who long for Him, not to those who pray for Him, and not to those who desire to be filled always; but He does give the Holy Spirit to them that obey Him." Indeed, the fullness of the Holy Spirit means to lose your life for Christ's sake (see Luke 9:24), and in that way to gain it in its fullest.

Some people think that I must be a very noble Corrie ten Boom to have been able to work in Germany and to forgive those who were very cruel to my family, even causing the deaths of some of them. But they do not understand that I, without Jesus Christ, could not love and help the German people. When Jesus tells us to love our enemies, He provides the love that He asks from us. Until we have loved our enemies, we have not tapped that love of which Jesus speaks. This means more than simply trying your hardest to be good. The truth is that God longs to give us the riches of His glory (see Ephesians 1:18). He is the only One from whom we can receive the power we need to be all that He wants us to be.

Jesus knocks at the door of our hearts, and when we open, He fills us with His joy, the fullness of the Holy Spirit, and the love of God.

Do not struggle to get out of rough hands. God uses rough hands to make us beautiful and perfect. Of Jesus we read: "The soldiers platted a crown of thorns, and put it on his head" (John 19:2 KJV). "I gave my back to the smiters, and . . . I hid not my face from shame and spitting" (Isaiah 50:6 KJV). He had power to help Himself, but He never used it.

27

He Brought the Word, Jesus

The Indian Christian, the Sadhu Sundar Singh, was once asked if he was influenced by the honor his friends gave him.

He said, "When Jesus entered Jerusalem, many people spread their clothing and palm branches on the street to honor the Lord.

"Jesus was riding, as the prophets foretold, on a donkey. In this way the feet of Jesus did not touch the street adorned with clothes and branches, but instead the donkey walked over them.

"It would have been very stupid of the donkey if she had imagined that she was very important. It was not for her that the people threw their clothes on the streets."

Stupid are those who spread the good news of Jesus and expect to receive glory themselves. The glory should go to Jesus.

The more people came to this godly man after his meetings, the more the Sadhu Sundar Singh withdrew from the crowd, to be in the silence where God spoke to him.

No sensation. No show.

He brought them the living Word, Jesus.

From the July 8th entry in *Each New Day* by Corrie ten Boom. Copyright © 1977.

28

God's Riches

"G od shall supply all your needs according to His riches in glory in Christ Jesus" (Philippians 4:19 NASB). When the Bible writers describe our riches in Jesus Christ, they often use words starting with "un": joy unspeakable (see 1 Peter 1:8), unsearchable riches (see Ephesians 3:8), and unspeakable gifts, (see 2 Corinthians 9:15). It seems as if they cannot find words to show the abundance the Lord gives us.

I think the reason is that the boundless resources of God's promises are celestial. They are earthly reproductions of heavenly riches in Jesus Christ, and they are ours under every circumstance.

All of His riches are for us—not to admire, but to take and keep. The antichrist is marching on and organizing his army over the whole world, but we stand on the Lord's side and may accept all His promises.

Too often we are like people who stand in front of the show window of a jewelry store. We admire the beautiful watches, rings, and bracelets, but we do not go in and pay the price in order to possess them. We just walk away! It is through Jesus that God's greatest and most precious promises have become available to us.

In my book *Plenty for Everyone,* I tell of a parable by F. B. Meyer, which describes a rich palace that is open to everyone who belongs to the Lord Jesus. Jesus is the door to the palace, and when we put our hands into His, He leads us from room to room.

The first room, rebirth:

"Except a man be born again, he cannot see the kingdom of God" (John 3:3 KJV).

The second room, assurance of salvation:

"You that believe on the name of the Son of God . . . may know that ye have eternal life" (1 John 5:13 KJV).

The third room, surrendered will:

"I delight to do thy will, O my God" (Psalm 40:8 KJV). Sometimes it seems so hard that we have to pray, "Lord make me willing to surrender my will."

The fourth room, total surrender:

"The price was in fact the lifeblood of Christ" (1 Peter 1:19 PHILLIPS).

The fifth room, the fullness of the Holy Spirit:

"Be filled with the Spirit" (Ephesians 5:18 KJV). Have you got the Holy Spirit? Has the Holy Spirit got you? Some people think the Spirit is for the spiritual aristocracy. But He is for every child of God.

The sixth room, abiding in Christ:

"Abide in him; that, when he shall appear, we may have confidence, and not be ashamed before him at his coming" (1 John 2:28 KJV).

The seventh room, victory over sin:

"Thanks be to God, which giveth us the victory through our Lord Jesus Christ" (1 Corinthians 15:57 KJV). Every child of God is to be an overcomer.

The eighth room, heart's rest:

"We . . . do not cease to pray for you, and to desire that ye might be filled with the knowledge of his will in all wisdom and spiritual understanding"

(Colossians 1:9 KJV). Rest in the Lord is independent of our external circumstances: It is a trusting, triumphant relationship with the Lord Himself.

If we live only in the first room, rebirth, we can be happy to realize that we are saved, but it is only the beginning. There is so much more available. The Bible tells us that there is a kingdom to build.

When Jesus reigns in our hearts, we have all the power necessary to build the kingdom. When we live like beggars, we are unhappy and do not enjoy the riches to which we have a legal right. Give Him the chance to multiply what He gives. Every child of God can live in all the rooms . . . for Jesus is alive and He is the door.

Just as you received Christ, so go on living in Him, in simple faith (see Colossians 2:6).

29

Apart from Him,
I Can Do Nothing

It is so tiring to hold the edge of my bed during the rolling of the ship that I fasten myself with a rope to my mattress. I am the only passenger on board the freighter, and I must share my cabin with the gyrocompass. I am a bad sailor and find sea travel a tribulation. Suddenly a huge wave hurls against the ship and I hear a strange sound. The gyrocompass whistles night and day, but now it is broken and the noise is peculiar. One of the engineers comes to repair it.

"Is this a bad storm?" I ask.

"Why, no! This is nothing at all. Wait until the wind force is fourteen, when we shall really know what rolling is."

At that moment, as if to contradict his words, a big wave throws the ship to one side. I hear the breaking of china, and everything that is not securely fastened runs from one side of the cabin to the other.

The storm has subsided by next morning, so I climb up to the bridge and meet the captain. After a chat about the weather, I say, "Captain, it is Sunday. May we have a church service?"

"What? A church service on my ship? It would be the first in my life!"

"Then," I reply with a smile, "it is high time you began, sir."

"All right. You can use the mess room. I am not opposed to the idea."

He himself writes on the notice board that at 11:00 A.M. there will be a church service in the mess room. At the appointed time nobody appears. The cabin boy brings me a cup of coffee. It is a Dutch ship, and the ship's cook knows that an 11:00 A.M. cup of coffee is a tradition.

"Are you going to stay?" I ask the boy. "I have a very interesting story to tell you."

"I don't want to hear that nonsense," he says. "I will not have anything to do with that Bible and God business." He feels very cocksure and leaves me alone.

I never saw so empty a church; just a cup of coffee and myself. I am not at all on fire for the Lord. Were I enthusiastic, I would go to the bridge and say, "Come along, gentlemen; you must help me fill the mess room. Send your men and boys." But I don't do that. I go to my cabin and am very seasick. That is the only thing I can do during the whole week.

Sunday comes around again. I am feeling discouraged and ashamed. "Lord, I am not a missionary. Send me back to my watchmaking business. I am not worthy to do Your work."

At that moment I find in my Bible a little piece of paper which I have never seen before. On it is written:

Cowardly, wayward, and weak,
I change with the changing sky,
Today so eager and strong,

Tomorrow not caring to try.
But He never gives in,
And we two shall win,
Jesus and I.

Instantly I see it! Indeed I am not worthy at all. The branch without the Vine cannot produce fruit, but I can do all things through Christ who gives me strength. The strongest and the weakest branches are worth nothing without the Vine; but connected to it they have the same nature. "As the branch cannot bear fruit of itself, except it abide in the vine; no more can ye, except ye abide in me" (John 15:4 KJV).

I go up to the bridge. "Captain, it is Sunday. Can we have a church service?"

"Again? In a church as empty as last week?" he asks teasingly.

"No, Captain. Not empty, but full, and you must help me."

He does, and there are ten men in the mess room. When my sermon is finished the cabin boy says, "It was not boring at all!"

We mutter and flutter, we fume and we spurt.
We mumble and grumble, our feelings get hurt.
We can't understand things, our vision gets dim,
When all that we need is a moment with Him.

30

※

Are You Free?

The reason for our lack of freedom can often be found in our past:

in a sin we committed
in forgiveness for and from people with whom we
    have or had a relationship
in bondage to wrong people
in bondage to right people

In a sin we committed. We look at our sins by means of two influences:

1. Satan is an accuser of the saints (see Revelation 12:10). He shows us our sins and brings us to despair. He tells us that this is the way we are and that there is no hope of change for us.

2. The Holy Spirit shows us our sins in the blessed floodlight of the finished work at the cross. He tells us Jesus died for these sins and bore the punishment and that He lives and is willing to make us more than conquerors. He cleanses us with His blood and gives us victory. We overcome by the blood of the Lamb and the word of our testimony (see Revelation 12:11). Jesus is

the answer, and by the Holy Spirit we are able to close our ears to the accuser.

In forgiveness for and from people with whom we have or had a relationship. I experienced the great miracle that I could forgive the murderers of my loved ones. I claimed Romans 5:5: "The love of God is shed abroad in our hearts by the Holy Ghost" (KJV). That is exactly the promise we must claim to be able to forgive! Never wait for people to ask forgiveness.

In bondage to wrong people. How the enemy will use human channels! The answer is to break the friendship in the power of Jesus Christ. We cannot be ready for His coming when we are not right with God and man.

In bondage to right people. I had to learn this myself. There was a work inspired by my sister Betsie who died in the concentration camp. She had shown me the work I should do after the war. I had to leave that work, and I felt very sad. There came a depression upon me. A sister in the Lord showed me that bondage to someone who had died could be wrong. I was set free in the name of Jesus, and the Lord gave me great peace.

"If the Son therefore shall make you free, ye shall be free indeed" (John 8:36 KJV).

31

To Prisoners

In the concentration camp where I was imprisoned many years ago, sometimes bitterness and hatred tried to enter my heart when people were so cruel to my sister and me. Then I learned this prayer, a "thank you" for Romans 5:5.

"Thank You, Lord Jesus, that You have brought into my heart the love of God through the Holy Spirit, who is given to me. Thank You, Father, that Your love in me is victorious over the bitterness in me and cruelty around me."

After I prayed it, I experienced the miracle that there was no room for bitterness in my heart any more. Will you learn to pray that prayer too?

If you are a child of God, you have a great task in your prison. You are a representative of the Lord Jesus, the King of kings (see 2 Corinthians 5:20). He will use you to win others for Christ. You can't? I can't either, but Jesus can.

The Bible says, "Be filled with the Spirit" (Ephesians 5:18 KJV). If you give room in your life to the Holy Spirit, then He can work through you, making you the salt of the earth and a shining light in your prison.

"In all these things we are more than conquerors through him that loved us" (Romans 8:37 KJV).

32

A Garden of the Lord

When you are a little bit old like I am, then you often remember very long ago. Perhaps seventy years ago, we had in Holland among the Christians an expression that said, "Don't forget Spurgeon." Spurgeon was an English evangelist of that time, and he wrote many books. And many times as I am enjoying my garden, a passage from Spurgeon comes back to me. It was something of a prayer.

"Oh, to have one's soul under heavenly cultivation, no wilderness, but a garden of the Lord, walled around by grace, planted by instruction, visited by love, weeded by heavenly discipline, and guarded by divine power. One's soul thus favored is prepared to yield fruit to the glory of God."

Isn't that beautiful? Have you ever thought of your life that way—as a garden of the Lord? When we receive Jesus Christ as our Savior, then at that moment each of us becomes a "garden of the Lord." As Spurgeon said, "not a wilderness, but a field under heavenly cultivation."

Of course, there are days without the sun when nothing seems to be growing! Our spiritual lives are barren— inside we feel that we are a real wilderness. When that attack comes, remember that the battle for the Christian is not against flesh and blood, but against the unseen powers of darkness. It is Satan's work to keep us from the Son—the only place where we can grow. The Bible makes it very clear that Satan will always be our accuser. But he is a liar! Lying is his main business.

God's Word gives us a different promise: "Where sin abounded, grace did much more abound" (Romans 5:20 KJV). That is what Spurgeon meant when he said that our gardens are walled around by grace!

My garden has a wood fence around it. The plants accept that their place is inside the fence. They know that is where they can grow. The answer to your and my sin problem is found in 2 Corinthians 12:9: "My grace is sufficient for you, for my power is made perfect in weakness" (RSV). God's grace in calling us to His Son can never be totally understood in this life, but it can be accepted.

This life has a way of separating us from the Savior's intensive care. Being self-occupied will kill the soil of our spiritual gardens. Jesus makes it clear that the way of self has to be finished. We must lose our lives for His sake to fully experience His power.

Does that mean that your "self" has to die? Yes. Many of the flowers in this garden were planted as seeds in the fall. In a way, that seed had to die to give birth to all this beauty!

The Holy Spirit does not tell you that you are strong or that you can do anything or everything if you have positive thinking. That is positive fantasy! The Holy Spirit tells us that we are nothing in ourselves. We are like gloves that are filled with a hand and that hand is the Holy Spirit. The joy is when we surrender to the Lord. He does the job to change our wilderness into His garden, and it is He who will make our lives fruitful in the kingdom. Do not expect the Gardener's full help unless you are fully dependent upon Him.

"Oh, to have one's soul under heavenly cultivation, no wilderness, but a garden of the Lord, walled around by grace, planted by instruction, visited by love, weeded by heavenly discipline, and guarded by divine power. One's soul thus favored is prepared to yield fruit to the glory of God."

Are you praying Spurgeon's prayer?

Living a Fruitful Life

The fruit of the Spirit is love, joy, peace, longsuffering, gentleness, goodness, faith, meekness, [self-control]" (Galatians 5:22–23 KJV).

Love is the love of Christ that passes knowledge.

Joy is the joy unspeakable and full of glory.

Peace is the peace that passes all understanding that Jesus promised when He said, "My peace I give to you."

Longsuffering is forgiving—even your enemies, just as Jesus forgave His enemies when He was on the cross.

Gentleness is the reproduction of the gentleness of Jesus.

Goodness is Christlikeness: a kindly disposition.

Faithfulness: The disciples were not always faithful. At the betrayal of Jesus in the garden they all forsook Him and fled. But when the Holy Spirit came down at Pentecost they all became faithful unto death.

Meekness is not the same as weakness. Nor is it a native fruit of the human heart. It is an exotic fruit of heaven.

Self-control is mastering the appetites and passions, particularly the sensual.

All this fruit can be seen in you, but only when you are in contact with the Vine.

34

When the Spirit Is Willing, but . . .

Forty years ago when Betsie and I stood in roll call in the concentration camp we often saw people from other barracks. We never could get close enough to tell them about the Lord Jesus, but we did pray for them, because every day many died.

Years later I met one of those ladies we prayed for. She first sent me her whole life story, and after reading it I knew that she did not know the One who could make her whole life new. She came to a meeting where I was speaking and afterwards called me and said, "I did not know that such a thing existed as what you told about. You must have a great faith."

"No," I answered, "I have not a great faith, but even though it is only as small as a mustard seed, my Messiah Jesus has said that it is sufficient. My faith is in a great God!"

"I wish I had a bit of your joy and peace," she said. "I cannot forgive the people who have been so cruel to me."

Then I told her she could have joy and peace . . . that all she had to do was ask Jesus Christ into her life. After

I showed her the way, and prayed with her, she accepted Jesus as her Lord.

How I love Romans 5:5. I use it often, and I shared it with her. She prayed, "Thank you, Jesus, for Romans 5:5, that you brought into my heart God's love through the Holy Spirit. Thank you, Father, that your love is victorious over my hatred."

I knew the Lord would perform that miracle and give her a spirit of forgiveness towards those who took her family away. With that same love you can forgive others, dear friends. Your own love runs out, but God's love is always available. It is an act of your will to use this tremendous love. What a joy!

The Lord opens doors and sets the prisoners free, not only people behind iron doors but also prisoners of sin, of bondage. John 8:36 tells us, "If the Son therefore shall make you free, ye shall be free indeed" (KJV).

Say, are you really free? If not, Jesus can liberate you. Lay your weak hand in His strong hand. He has said, "Come unto me all who are heavy laden. I will give you rest."

There are moments when I am dead tired. Do you know how that feels? One day I felt like I was at the end, and I started to resent all the travel, the letters, and many other things. One morning when I was lying in bed I talked it over with the Lord. The Lord showed me, through the Holy Spirit, that I had the sin of resentment. I had started to argue when I remembered that Jesus cannot cleanse an excuse, so I confessed my sin and told the Lord I was willing to do whatever He had for me.

My joy became so full when I read in *The Living Bible,* Ephesians 3:14–19:

When I think of the wisdom and scope of his plan I fall down on my knees and pray to the Father of all the great family of God—some of them already in heaven and some down here on earth—that out of his glorious, unlimited resources he will give you the mighty inner strengthening of his Holy Spirit. And I pray that Christ will be more and more at home in your hearts, living within you as you trust in him. May your roots go down deep into the soil of God's marvelous love; and may you be able to feel and understand, as all God's children should, how long, how wide, how deep, and how high his love really is; and to experience this love for yourselves, though it is so great that you will never see the end of it or fully know or understand it. And so at last you will be filled up with God himself.

That encouraged me to know and trust that the unlimited resources of His strength are more than sufficient. I started to praise and thank the Lord, and my tiredness disappeared.

His unchanging plan has always been to adopt us into his own family by sending Jesus Christ to die for us. And he did this because he wanted to! Now all praise to God for his wonderful kindness to us and his favor that he has poured out upon us, because we belong to his dearly loved Son.

Ephesians 1:5–6 TLB

35

Learning to Forgive

It was in a church in Munich that I saw him, a balding heavyset man in a gray overcoat, a brown felt hat clutched between his hands. People were filing out of the basement room where I had just spoken, moving along the rows of wooden chairs to the door at the rear. It was 1947 and I had come from Holland to defeated Germany with the message that God forgives.

It was the truth they needed most to hear in that bitter, bombed-out land, and I gave them my favorite mental picture. Maybe because the sea is never far from a Hollander's mind, I liked to think that that's where forgiven sins were thrown. "When we confess our sins," I said, "God casts them into the deepest ocean, gone forever."

The solemn faces stared back at me, not quite daring to believe. There were never questions after a talk in Germany in 1947. People stood up in silence, in silence collected their wraps, in silence left the room.

And that's when I saw him, working his way forward against the others. One moment I saw the overcoat and the brown hat; the next, a blue uniform and a visored cap with its skull and crossbones. It came back with a rush:

the huge room with its harsh overhead lights, the pathetic pile of dresses and shoes in the center of the floor, the shame of walking naked past this man. I could see my sister's frail form ahead of me, ribs sharp beneath the parchment skin. Betsie, how thin you were!

Betsie and I had been arrested for concealing Jews in our home during the Nazi occupation of Holland; this man had been a guard at Ravensbrück concentration camp where we were sent.

Now he was in front of me, hand thrust out: "A fine message, *Fräulein!* How good it is to know that, as you say, all our sins are at the bottom of the sea!"

And I, who had spoken so glibly of forgiveness, fumbled in my pocketbook rather than take that hand. He would not remember me, of course—how could he remember one prisoner among those thousands of women?

But I remembered him and the leather crop swinging from his belt. It was the first time since my release that I had been face to face with one of my captors and my blood seemed to freeze.

"You mentioned Ravensbrück in your talk," he was saying. "I was a guard in there." No, he did not remember me.

"But since that time," he went on, "I have become a Christian. I know that God has forgiven me for the cruel things I did there, but I would like to hear it from your lips as well. *Fräulein*—" again the hand came out—"will you forgive me?"

And I stood there—I whose sins had every day to be forgiven—and could not. Betsie had died in that place—

could he erase her slow terrible death simply for the asking?

It could not have been many seconds that he stood there, hand held out, but to me it seemed hours as I wrestled with the most difficult thing I had ever had to do.

For I had to do it—I knew that. The message that God forgives has a prior condition: that we forgive those who have injured us. "If you do not forgive men their trespasses," Jesus says, "neither will your Father in heaven forgive your trespasses" (see Matthew 6:14–15).

I knew it not only as a commandment of God, but as a daily experience. Since the end of the war I had had a home in Holland for victims of Nazi brutality. Those who were able to forgive their former enemies were able also to return to the outside world and rebuild their lives, no matter what the physical scars. Those who nursed bitterness remained invalids. It was as simple and as horrible as that.

And still I stood there with the coldness clutching my heart. But forgiveness is not an emotion—I knew that too. Forgiveness is an act of the will, and the will can function regardless of the temperature of the heart. "Jesus, help me!" I prayed silently. "I can lift my hand. I can do that much. You supply the feeling."

And so woodenly, mechanically, I thrust my hand into the one stretched out to me. And as I did, an incredible thing took place. The current started in my shoulder, raced down my arm, sprang into our joined hands. And then this healing warmth seemed to flood my whole being, bringing tears to my eyes.

"I forgive you, brother!" I cried. "With all my heart!"

For a long moment we grasped each other's hands, the former guard and the former prisoner. I had never known God's love so intensely as I did then.

For because he himself has suffered and been tempted, he is able to help those who are tempted.

Hebrews 2:18 RSV

36

Bearing One Another's Burdens

What a joy it is to know that the Holy Spirit leads us when we have an opportunity to counsel people. When we need help, we can cash the check given in James 1:5: "If any of you lacks wisdom, let him ask God, who gives to all men generously and without reproaching, and it will be given him" (RSV).

I once had a talk with a student who suffered from nervous tension. Although the Lord performed a miracle of liberation, the boy still seemed rather absentminded. Then the Lord guided my approach to him.

"Will you do something for me?" I asked. "I have a problem. My prayer time is so attacked by the enemy. As soon as I start to pray, all kinds of thoughts start to distract me.

"There was a time in my life when unclean thoughts came into my heart the moment I would concentrate on praying. But this is past. Now they are clean, practical questions, such as, 'At what time must I speak tomorrow? Who is taking care of transportation? Are there enough vegetables and potatoes for Sunday?' All very good thoughts, but they hinder my concentration for prayer. Will you pray with me that the Lord will make me free and protect my prayer time?"

He did, and his prayer was something unusual—so dedicated, so understanding, so full of love. He showed a real burden for my problem!

"I am sure you have a ministry of intercession," I told him.

"I believe it, too," he answered.

At that moment I saw that his absentmindedness was gone. He was free. He became a real prayer partner from that day on. The moment he started to do something for another, he was free from self, with all its complications. And my prayer life was healed.

Another ministry of the Holy Spirit, I have discovered, is revealing our sins to us. While traveling around the world and meeting so many Christians, I found two attitudes toward sin. One is the easy way: "I am just human. Nobody is perfect." The other puts people under a permanent burden about past and present sins, not realizing the finished work of Jesus Christ on the cross.

In the power of the Lord Jesus Christ we stand on victory ground. He has lifted us out of the old vicious circle of sin and death (see Romans 8:2). From the circle of sinning, fighting, and conquering but always sinning again, fighting, failing, and so on, Jesus has brought us inside His blessed circle of repentance, forgiveness, and cleansing by His blood (see 1 John 1:7, 9).

The devil is not yet on pension! He is very active, but he is no longer victorious in the "blessed circle" where Jesus Christ has placed us. Whom Jesus makes free is free indeed, but to live this victorious life you must not leave the confessing of your sins until later. The door of repentance is wide open. Hallelujah!

It may be true what the scoffer says,

that the devil is dead and gone.
But sensible people would like to know
who carries the business on.

We will see more and more that we are chosen not
because of our ability, but because of His power that will
be demonstrated in our not being able.

37

Awakening to God's Peace

In Corrie's thirty-three years of traveling, she experienced many once-in-a-lifetime events. While traveling in India, she had the opportunity to take a trip on an elephant, and upon her return she wrote her impressions of that journey.

I used to have the idea that a jungle meant wild life full of thrills and surprises—a wild west experience. It is quite different. Of course, in jungle life wild beasts do kill each other and the struggle for life is constant and brutal, but I saw another side of the picture.

We arose very early in the morning after sleeping in a forest bungalow on top of a hill in the jungle. It was five o'clock when we started our trip. Our party was divided on the backs of two elephants.

It was dark in the jungle and we were quiet, for we hoped to see wild animals. If they hear voices they keep their distance, so the only noise was the breaking of branches under the feet of our elephants.

It was like a dream. Far in the east there seemed to come a light; the breath and whisper of dawn brought a promise of the coming day. The birds started singing and whistling—different from any whistling I had ever heard before. The jungle was awakening.

Slowly, very slowly, we moved through the wild woods. Sometimes the man in front of us would cut away the branches that could hurt us. It was all so peaceful, so quiet and restful.

This was enjoying nature—no hurry, for time does not count. Deer passed us at a short distance. They were not afraid of us, because we had become a part of the jungle for them. It became lighter and we could see the monkeys high up in the trees jumping from one treetop to another, odd fellows, full of mischief.

The sky in the east colored beautifully, and it was chilly. It reminded me of the coldness we felt at roll call in the concentration camp. I learned then that the coldest time of the day is about twenty minutes before sunrise, when the temperature drops.

I thought of the great change in my life. Then I was prisoner. Now I was free, so free that I could go around the world, even through a jungle in India. I felt so happy with my blessed life. There was a kind of heavenly joy in my heart, for I thought of the time when the sun of righteousness shall shine upon the earth and "the earth shall be full of the knowledge of the LORD, as the waters cover the sea" (Isaiah 11:9 KJV). I experienced a foretaste of the time when there will be peace on earth as there now is in heaven.

Suddenly, as the sunbeams shot through the trees, it was as if life increased in the jungle, and we began to see more animals. Two men who were walking noiselessly before us gave us a sign to stop. They looked at the footprints on the ground and whispered, "Bison." The elephants stood motionless. Then we saw them, a herd of twenty, thirty, perhaps even forty bison! They also saw us, and gazing curiously in our direction, they too stood motionless.

What did they intend to do? I told myself that if they should come and surround us, the elephants would become unruly and throw us down. But I could not think of panic. This was all so natural and peaceful; and even if something were to happen, why fear? The best is yet to be!

The bison turned and moved away. Carefully the elephants stepped down into a little steep valley. It is wonderful how these enormous animals can walk so securely on a small path, even up and down, feeling their way with the tips of their trunks.

How well I would remember this jungle. When I was in the midst of the noise of the big cities, when I had to find my way through the jungle of Times Square in New York City or the Ginza Nishu in Tokyo, it helped me to know that there are jungles where there is an abundance of time, quietness, and beautiful nature and where it is possible to travel only six miles in four hours, as we did. Here our eyes grasped more and enjoyed beauty that would never be seen during the thousands of miles traveled at high speeds in airplanes and automobiles.

The elephants knelt down. It was the end of our trip. Some black hands kindly helped me to the ground, and I felt as refreshed as if I had had two weeks' vacation.

Where there is faith, there is love
Where there is love, there is peace
Where there is peace, there is blessing

Where there is blessing, there is God
Where there is God, there is no want.

Surely I have composed and quieted my soul;
Like a weaned child rests against his mother,
My soul is like a weaned child within me.

Psalm 131:2 NASB

38

Our Hands in His

Sometimes the responsibility of all my work has burdened me. There is so much to do, and we all understand that we must redeem the time, because the days are evil (see Ephesians 5:16). What joy that we may and must surrender everything.

When I talked over my concern with the Lord, He showed me an empty suitcase. He said: "You possess nothing; you have surrendered all, so you have no responsibilities at all. I carry all responsibilities; you are only My steward."

What joy came into my heart! I prayed, "O Lord, let me see You a moment."

"Look at your left hand," He said. I saw that my hand was in another hand. That hand was pierced . . . it was Jesus' hand. I never before understood what surrender meant—our weak hand in Jesus' strong hand! His strength in our life! Surrender to the Lord Jesus is dynamic and relaxed. What joy! Hallelujah!

39

Look to Jesus

G od is able to make all grace abound toward you; that ye, always having all sufficiency in all things, may abound to every good work" (2 Corinthians 9:8 KJV).

In Germany I once spoke to young people about the riches we possess in Christ Jesus. Germans are reticent, and when I asked them to stay for an after-talk, only seven remained. Soon we broke the ice.

One said, "I am an atheist. You do it with Jesus, I do it without Him and just as well." When he told of what he had achieved in his own strength, I did not say much. I am not much good at arguing. Silently I prayed for him while listening, and then I said, "Should there ever come a time in your life when you cannot work in your own strength, then think of what you heard tonight."

Then another young man began to talk, and he said, "Once I was a soldier of Hitler; now I am a soldier of Jesus. To me the Bible is an accounting of all I possess in Him. I followed Hitler wholeheartedly; God struck everything out of my hands. I was in prison, and in that prison camp a comrade read the Bible with me every day. Then I saw."

From *Amazing Love* by Corrie ten Boom, 46–47. Copyright © 1953.

After that, the others told of their difficulties. One girl said, "I am so unfaithful. I am willing, but my faith is so unequal. Now that you have told me so much, I feel certain, but tomorrow? I don't know whether I shall succeed then."

"When I was a watchmaker, sometimes I had new watches that did not run well," I told her. "I did not repair them myself, but returned them to the manufacturer. When he had repaired them, they ran perfectly. This is what I do with my faith. Jesus is the Author and Finisher of our faith. If it does not work well, I return it to the heavenly Manufacturer. And when He has repaired it, it works perfectly!"

Let us look more and more at Jesus, not at our faith. Let us not consider the gales around us, but Him; then we can walk on the waves. Faith is such a firm ground that the safest path to walk on is the sea which Peter walked towards Jesus.

Of itself, our conversation changed into a prayer meeting. The "atheist" also folded his hands and closed his eyes.

40

∞∞∞

From the Old Chest

My nephew, Peter van Woerden, and I wrote a book dealing with our ancestry, and much of the material was taken from letters and documents found in an old chest. There were many interesting items in that chest!

Here is a letter I wrote in 1916 to some of my friends.

January 30, 1916

Dear Girls,

Last night I had an interesting dream. Before I forget it, I want to tell you all about it. It was so exciting. The funny thing was that all during my dream I was conscious that these things were happening many, many years before I was born. It was the time when my great-grandfather Gerrit was a gardener in the Bronstede Estate. Father has often told me about this man's faith, courage, and patriotism. Now, here is my dream.

I was walking over a rough street with cobblestones and thought I had never had such an interesting adventure. The people I saw had different clothing from what I had on. Old-fashioned carriages passed me—a

This letter was first published, in part, in *Father ten Boom: God's Man* by Corrie ten Boom, 116–17. Copyright © 1978. The paragraph following the letter is from page 22 of the same publication.

long train of gigs with many horses in front. I realized that I walked there in the time when the princes of Orange still reigned in our country.

I saw an old inn at the side of the road. I went in and saw an interior like a Frans Hals painting: men sitting there with broad brimmed hats on, smoking pipes and sitting on rough chairs beside windows with small window panes. But the birds outside were singing just as in our time. The trees and flowers were not different from ours.

I did not say anything, but the people seemed to know who I was and the innkeeper said, "That man over there is Master ten Boom. I am sure you are interested in meeting him."

My forefather greeted me kindly but did not seem amazed to see someone who would live a hundred years later. "Come with me," he said. "My wife will be glad to meet you."

On the way to his home we did not talk much, but when I saw the old-fashioned carriages I said, "Perhaps I could visit the prince of Orange; he certainly would like to meet someone who will live many years after today."

"That would take much, much time," Great-grandfather said. "The prince lives in the Hague. How are you going to get there?" I suddenly realized that there were not yet any trains or automobiles. It would take me days to get there.

Very quickly we were in the kitchen where Great-grandmother was cooking a meal. They sat down at the table to eat, and I sat next to the window. A boy of about ten took off his cap and they all prayed silently. "Is that boy my grandfather?" I thought to myself. After the meal, Great-grandfather took his Bible and read a portion.

"Child," he said, "when your time to live comes, much

will be different from what you see here around you. But this Book will be the same. If anyone undertakes to change it, then know that it is wrong. The Word of God is the same forever and ever."

He took my hand and led me to the garden. I saw how he put some seed into the earth. "This seed will give flowers. Before they die they will give seed. And so it will go on. In your days, there will still be flowers that come forth from this seed. In the same way it will go with the ten Booms. You will exist many years after I shall have died."

This was the end of my dream, but I was strangely moved. I like what I have dreamed about the Bible. "Heaven and earth will pass away, but God's Word will never pass away." I only doubt if I will ever enjoy a new translation.

God bless you girls,
Your Corrie

We are surrounded by a cloud of witnesses.

Great-grandfather Gerrit's life was one of those seeds that was to bear fruit later. In one of the letters his house was referred to as "a house of prayer." Some thirty years after his death, the church in Heemstede became the scene of a fresh revival under the ministry of a godly pastor, Nicolaas Beets. Gerrit's prayers and tears had not been in vain. The lessons of history teach us patience. As a Dutch saying has it, "God's mills often grind slowly, but they grind surely."

Away with work that hinders prayer,
    'twere best to lay it down.
For prayerless work, however good,
    will fail to win the crown.

41

God's Special People

Before World War II began, Corrie was involved in working to bring the gospel to mentally handicapped people. She later wrote a booklet about these experiences entitled *Common Sense Not Needed*. The following stories are excerpts from that booklet.

Bringing the gospel to mentally handicapped people is not important work in the eyes of the world. To convert a "big shot" is more important than to save a mentally handicapped person who cannot organize a mission, cannot start a drive to collect money, cannot write books, and cannot do what splendid, gifted Christians can.

Does heaven have the same standards as earth? I do not think so.

I believe that the joy of the angels of God when a handicapped person is converted is as great as when a "big shot" gives his heart and life to Jesus. It is possible that the joy is greater; heaven is different from earth. One can never tell.

From *Common Sense Not Needed* by Corrie ten Boom, 25–26, 28. Copyright © 1957.

I had spoken to our boys about prayer. Jake, the tramp, accompanied me home. (My friends often said, "Such dignified friends you walk around with!") First he told me how he had set up in his business. He had taken the door off his room and chopped it up into small pieces to make firewood. He had sold the wood, going from door to door. This was good business in Holland during the war. Cost: not one cent. Profit: enough money for many weeks. It was not easy to persuade Jake that what he did was stealing.

"Jake, do you know what prayer is?" I asked.

At first he was silent.

"Do you mean like this?" Jake asked hesitatingly. "Often I feel something I can't push away."

"That's it, Jake! Praying is asking Jesus to push away what you cannot push yourself. Jesus can do everything and He loves you so much that He wants to push away the bad things in your life."

Next day *I* had something *I* could not "push away." I was downhearted and the spirit of worry was in my heart. Then I remembered the conversation with Jake and I asked, "Lord Jesus, will you push away the worry?"

And He did.

Anton was a Mongoloid. He could neither speak nor walk alone. He was in my class for a very short time. He listened to my Bible stories, but when I spoke too long to suit him, he yawned. . . . I did not know how much Anton really understood.

Once I took his hand and touched his five fingers one after another and said, "Jesus loves Anton so much." The next week, when Anton saw me, he took my hand and with his fingers outspread, looked at me with a face full of longing. "Jesus loves Anton so much," I repeated, touching a finger at every word. Then I taught him to do it himself.

After that, every week, Anton showed me with his fingers how much Jesus loved him. The last time I saw him, I told him while he touched his left fingers with his right hand, "Jesus loves Anton so much. How thankful I am for that! You too, Anton?"

"Yes," Anton said, as his face lit up.

It was the only word I ever heard from Anton. It is the most worthwhile word that any person can speak to the Lord Jesus.

42

Choices

Several years ago I was in Vietnam. It was one of the times I suffered with the people in the war. I remember that I went as far as I could go through the jungle and rice paddies to the front lines so I could speak to the American G.I.'s—young men, yes, in my eyes still boys. Their life was hard. Days and days they had to live in the jungle. They suffered and made people suffer.

We heard around us bombs falling and the "ric-a-tic" of machine guns. The soldiers were thankful—almost too happy—for a visit from an old lady who had come from a country where there was peace. And now I was with them on the battlefield. They seldom saw women there, perhaps only the prostitutes. I had such pity for them.

I tried first to tell them all the jokes I could remember in English. Then I said, "Now boys, I want to talk 'turkey.'" (I tried to use some slang I had learned from the students.) "There are two possibilities. Either you come through the war alive or you fall in action. Let us think a moment if that last thing happens. Are you ready to meet a righteous God? Are you not ready? Come to Jesus. He is willing and able to prepare you."

A lady told me later that her son had written her from Vietnam: "Now I know what it means to receive Jesus Christ as my Savior. I did it and what peace there is in my heart." Three weeks later he fell in action.

43

When Will Jesus Come?

Can we expect that Jesus will return soon? I think we can, and I am looking forward to it, full of expectation. What a joy when He will do that which He promises in Revelation 21:5: "I make all things new."

Will God's children have to pass through the great tribulation? Many expect that we shall be taken away before it comes. But now already there is a terrible battle going on between the powers of the kingdom of light and those of the kingdom of darkness. Is not every Christian more or less on the front line? But we know that those who are with us are much stronger and more numerous than those who are against us.

What joy to know that Jesus said, "In the world ye shall have tribulation: but be of good cheer; I have overcome the world" (John 16:33 KJV). And when the situation grows worse and worse and our hearts nearly faint for fear, will not then the time have come to "look up, and lift up your heads; for your redemption draweth nigh" (Luke 21:28 KJV)?

The world needs strong and trusting Christians, especially during the time of tribulation. It needs Christians who see the reality of God's plan and of Jesus' victory.

"Where there is no vision, the people perish" (Proverbs 29:18 KJV).

For each one personally it will be very important whether the Lord Jesus is our Judge or our Savior. Do not wait to accept Him; do it now. One day it will be too late.

I do not know when Jesus will come again. I do not know the hour or the day, but I know that He will come and that there is no hour or day when He could not come.

> And now, . . . abide in him; that, when he shall appear, we may have confidence, and not be ashamed before him at his coming.
>
> *1 John* 2:28 KJV

Not Good If Detached

Corrie ten Boom

Guideposts®

CARMEL, NEW YORK 10512

www.guidepostsbooks.com

This Guideposts edition is published by special arrangement with
Revell, a division of Baker Book House Company.

© 1966 by Christians, Incorporated

Published by Fleming H. Revell
a division of Baker Book House Company
P.O. Box 6287, Grand Rapids, MI 49516-6287

Printed in the United States of America

Library of Congress Cataloging-in-Publication Data
Ten Boom, Corrie.
    Not good if detached / Corrie ten Boom.
       p. cm.—(Corrie ten Boom library)
    ISBN 0-8007-1765-1 (cloth)
    1. Ten Boom, Corrie. 2. Christian biography. I. Title. II. Series.
BR1725.T35A3 1999
269p.2p092—dc21   98-46635

Unless otherwise indicated, Scripture quotations are from the King James Version of the Bible.

Scripture quotations identified PHILLIPS are from The New Testament in Modern English (revised edition), translated by J. B. Phillips. © J. B. Phillips 1958, 1960, 1972. Used by permission of Macmillan Publishing Co., Inc.

For current information about all releases from Baker Book House, visit our Web site: www.bakerbooks.com

Interior design by Holly Johnson
Front cover design by Cathy Kovacs/Enterprise Four
Back cover design by Dennis Arnold
Typeset by Composition Technologies, Inc.

Contents

Contents

Preface

Corrie ten Boom is one of those rare souls whose experience with God has been so different from that of other Christians that it must be described as unique. Brought up in the staid surroundings of a Reformed household and church in the Netherlands, her life was uneventful. Came the war, and Corrie with her family decided to succor the helpless Jewish victims of Gestapo terror without stopping to count the cost to herself. Had she known that it would take the lives of her nearest and dearest, she might have flinched. So merciful Providence hid the future from her, until she could live it one day at a time.

In *A Prisoner and Yet . . .* she tells of her walk with God through the valley of the shadow of an imminent death in Ravensbrück concentration camp. When unexpectedly released, a living skeleton, she quietly determined to carry out her vow to witness around the world to the grace of God.

Amazing Love tells of her postwar experiences far afield and shows the maturing of her Christian service. It has been my privilege to know Corrie ten Boom and her ministry for several years, and a greater privilege still to have had her as a true yoke-fellow in the ministry in several of the continents. I do not know of anyone more earnestly seeking to be "one hundred percent for God"—which is her own phrase to describe a fully yielded life.

This book is written in Corrie's own style. Although her friends agree that she is always willing to learn, there are certain things that they cease trying to change; one of them being Corrie's style of writing and utterance. It is her own, and it is unique. It reflects her mind and her heart.

I commend to you our sister Corrie, a servant of the church at large, that you may receive her in the Lord as befits the saints and help her in whatever she may require from you, for she has been a helper of many and of myself as well.

In connection with this book, all that Corrie ten Boom requires of the reader is that this volume be read with a heart open for blessing.

J. Edwin Orr

1

Three African Boys

The world is our mission-field, for it is Jesus' mission-field.

In a prison in Africa, forty boys are sitting on the concrete floor of their cell. They listen while I tell them about the promise of the second coming of Jesus. After a meeting in the prison square, they had asked to hear more. There they had been sitting with all the prisoners packed closely together, hundreds of boys, most of them younger than eighteen years, and many guilty of theft or murder. I had told them how Jesus lifted us up out of sin and death when He died for us. I barely mentioned the future, when this world shall be full of the knowledge of the Lord, as the waters cover the sea (Isaiah 11:9). When Jesus comes, He has promised He will "make all things new" (Revelation 21:5).

The boys sleep on the cold floor of the cell. One boy puts his blanket on the little stool where I am to sit. It is all he possesses. An evangelist who regularly works among them is my interpreter, and he leads the prayer meeting that follows.

Several boys pray.

A sunbeam touches the face of a boy who prays on his

knees, with his head uplifted. There is the peace that passes all understanding on his black face. He is seventeen years old and was the leader of a gang.

In a small crowded prison Christians who bravely dare to witness have a difficult life. He is one who witnesses. I do not understand his language. Does he pray, "Come, Lord Jesus, come quickly"?

When leaving, I tell him and two others, "Just imagine that you saw Jesus coming there on those clouds up in heaven." There is longing and expectation on their eager faces when they look up.

There is coming a moment in history when that which is written of in Revelation 22:17 will take place. "And the Spirit and the bride say, 'Come.' And let him that heareth say, 'Come.' And let him that is athirst come. And whosoever will, let him take the water of life freely."

I am called to distribute that "water of life" in many countries.

In this book you will read about what God did with one of His children on several trips throughout the world. The experiences are so personal that the dangerous word "I" is used too often. But it is my only wish to seek to honor Him who is my Lord, Jesus Christ, God's Son.

The branch of the Vine can only give fruit through Him. Without Him we can do nothing. The riches in Him are so great and full of joy. He is the only answer to the problem of the hearts of men.

But we have this treasure in a "common earthenware jar"—to show that the splendid power of it belongs to God and not to us. For it is Christ the Lord whom we preach, and not ourselves (2 Corinthians 4:7, 5 PHILLIPS).

In this book are told some of the things that happened

to a "common earthenware jar." It is the treasure that is important, not the jar.

At the time of writing this book I have been traveling for ten years. Up to my fiftieth year I had always lived in one town—Haarlem, in the Netherlands. Then the cruel hand of war destroyed the quiet life of our happy family. The foundation of our happiness was that we knew ourselves hidden with Christ in God. The enemy could take away our material possessions, but he could not destroy our faith in God's love in Jesus Christ.

On the contrary, when all earthly security was very uncertain, we experienced with tremendous joy the invincibility of the sure Rock to which our anchor is eternally fastened. Before, we had believed, but now we knew that the light of Jesus Christ is stronger than the deepest darkness.

First there were the years of intensive work in the underground movement to save Jewish people. Then came the arrest and imprisonment of my whole family, which, for all except myself, ended in death. For me it ended in being called to be a "tramp for the Lord" over the whole world. *"Une troubadoure de Dieu."*

My sister Betsie, who was with me in the concentration camp, had a vision. She awakened me in the middle of the night to share it with me. "Corrie, God has spoken to me. When we are free, we must do two things. We must open a house for these prisoners around us. Those who come out alive will have a difficult time to find their way through life again. They are morally wounded. God will give us a beautiful big house, and many will be healed there. But we must not stay there. We must travel over the whole world. We have a message for the world. From experience we can now tell that a child of God can never go so deep into darkness that he will not always find beneath him the everlasting arms that uphold him."

A week later Betsie died. Shortly after that I was set free. I started the two things that God had shown to Betsie.

The house for ex-prisoners was opened in Bloemendaal less than a year after I came out of prison. It is now an international center operated by the ten Boom Foundation as a home for those who need rest and relaxation. The war-weary people are back in their own homes again, and now many guests from Holland and from other lands spend their vacation in the beautiful house, "Zonneduin" ("Sunny Dune House").*

In my book *Amazing Love* I cover some of my experiences traveling in many countries. In an earlier book, *A Prisoner and Yet . . .* I describe what happened to my life in underground work and in prison camps during the war.

In this third book I have included some things I have learned through meeting a great variety of people around the world, but more of the things He has taught me who said, "Lo, I am with you alway, even unto the end of the world."

Connected with Him in His love, I am more than conqueror; without Him, I am nothing. Like some railway tickets in America, I am "not good if detached."

---

*1973—Zonneduin is now a house for convalescents who still need care and treatment. The Dutch Reformed Church has taken over its direction.

2

———⚬⚬⚬———

First Steps on a World Tour

Teach me Thy way, O LORD.

Psalm 27:11

Now I am about to obey the second half of God's commission. He has told me to go to America, but I find that many papers are needed. I must visit so many offices. This is the first difficult test of obedience to the guidance upon which I now depend. When my parents were married they were given the verse, "I will instruct thee and teach thee in the way which thou shalt go: I will guide thee with Mine eye" (Psalm 32:8). This promise becomes my special directive for all my journeyings.

Wherever I go, the answer is, "No papers are available for America."

I pray, "Lord if it is Your will that I go to America, they must provide papers." Again and again God performs a miracle. After some time I have most of the papers in my hand.

Man's importunity is God's opportunity. He uses our problems as building materials for His miracles. These are my first steps on the path to complete dependence on the obedience to His guidance. How much I still have to learn!

At last I have all my papers except one. The worst obstacle seems to await me at the tenth office. Everyone coming out warns those of us waiting in the hall, "That fellow in there is as hard as flint; he passes no one." I have to wait a long time.

Three ladies and a gentleman pass me. One of the ladies stops. "Hello there! Don't we know each other? Aren't you a cousin of mine?" We have not seen each other for years. She introduces her husband.

I ask, "Are you, too, planning to go to America?"

"Not at all. My office is in this building."

"Then perhaps you can help me," and I tell him my story.

"I'm sorry; I'd like to be of service to my brand-new cousin, but that's not in my department. However, if you have trouble, ring me up." And he gives me his office telephone number.

Time passes, and the "man of stone" goes out for coffee. A very young clerk takes his place. When my turn comes he says, "You had better wait until my boss returns."

"No! I can't wait any longer. Won't you please call this number?"

I give him the telephone number of my cousin. The side of the conversation I hear is encouraging. Hanging up the telephone, he says, "Yes, you may have your papers." The miracle has happened. Now for ship reservations.

In Amsterdam I try to arrange my passage on a ship of the Holland-America line. I am told, "We'll put your name on the waiting list and call you when there is room. It may take ten or twelve months."

Surely that cannot be true! It has been made so plain to me that I must go *now*.

Disappointed, I stand in the Square and notice that the American Express Company has opened an office. I might try for a berth on a freighter. Stepping into the office, I inquire, "Have you passenger accommodation on freighters to America?"

"You may sail tomorrow, madam, if your papers are in order."

"But tomorrow is too sudden. What about next week?"

"That, too, can be arranged."

So I come to America. New York is a great city. The skyscrapers are so very tall, and Corrie ten Boom is so very small. Fifty dollars is all I have taken with me; more is not permitted. But there are two checks in my pocket. While still in Holland I had told my plans to an American visiting relatives there. Shaking his head, he had warned me that it was not easy to make one's way in America.

"I believe you, but God has directed me and I must obey."

He had given me a large check and a smaller one. "If you need them, use them, and you can repay me later."

In New York a YWCA provides me with a room for one week. I speak that week to several groups of Jewish Christian immigrants. Since they are German, I cannot use the English lectures I have prepared while on board ship.

When I pay the rent for my room at the end of the week the clerk asks where she should send my suitcases.

"I am unable to say at present," I reply.

"I am so sorry, but our accommodation is so limited that we cannot allow you to stay here any longer."

"Yes, I know, but God has another room for me. It is just that I don't know the address."

She looks perplexed, but I am not worried. God led me through Ravensbrück! He will surely see me through America.

Then suddenly she recalls, "There is a letter for you."

How can that be, since nobody knows where I am staying? But there it is.

I read the letter, and say, "My suitcases go to this address," and I give her the number of a house on 190th Street.

"But why didn't you tell me that before?"

"I didn't know. It's in this letter. A woman writes, 'I heard you speak this week to the Jewish congregation. I am aware that it is almost impossible to get a room in New York City. My son happens to be in Europe, so you are welcome to use his room as long as you are staying in New York.'"

The lady at the desk is more amazed than I am. Perhaps she has not experienced as many miracles as I have.

The subway takes me to 190th Street. It is a large house occupied by many families. At the end of a hall is the number I am looking for, but my hostess is away. She certainly could not have expected her invitation to be an eleventh-hour answer to my problem. Arranging myself among my suitcases, I soon fall asleep, for I am tired. Thus she finds me when she returns after midnight, and I become her guest for five weeks.

Five weeks that test my faith. One check has already been cashed. Jan ten Have, the publisher of my books in Holland, is in New York. He is a faithful friend and helps me as much as he can. My time is spent looking up addresses given me in Holland and telling my experiences. The Americans are friendly and say my story is interesting. They will keep me in mind, but they are unable to arrange meetings for me at present. However, they give me some more names. I call on these also. Not all are polite. Some even say I should have stayed in Holland.

"Why did you come to America?" so many ask.

"God has directed me and I can only obey," is my reply.

"That's nonsense. There is no such thing as direct guidance from God. Experience proves that you must use your common sense."

"Sure I must use my common sense, but God's guidance is even more important, and I am certain I have to bring a message here. I can declare that the deepest darkness is outshone by the light of Jesus."

"We have our ministers to tell us such things."

"Certainly; but I can tell from my experiences in a concentration camp that what the ministers say is true."

"It would have been better for you to have remained in Holland. Too many Europeans come to America. They should be stopped."

Are they right? My money is all gone, except the larger check. I do not want to cash it before seeing the man who gave it to me. I find his address and arrive in an imposing business office. His face is no longer so friendly.

"Do you mind if I cash your other check?" I ask.

"How do I know if or when you can return my money? Have not five weeks in America been long enough to prove there is no work here for you? Please return my check."

He writes me another bearing a much smaller amount.

Mustering all my courage, I say, "I am sure God has work here for me. I am in His will and will soon return your money."

I am embarrassed and humbled. I have money in Holland—a balance left from my first book, and a small income from the business I sold—but these funds cannot be brought to America.

In my room I have a long consultation with my heavenly Father, reciting all my troubles.

"Father, you must help me out," I pray. "If I must borrow money to return to Holland people will say, 'There, you see, the promises of the Bible are not really meant. Direct guidance does not exist.' Father, for Your own honor's sake, You must help me out."

The answer is clear. "Do not worry about My honor. I will take care of that. In days to come you will give thanks for these days in New York."

A great burden is lifted from my soul.

When I awake the next day the thought that a great ocean separates me from my homeland oppresses me, as it has every morning since coming here. All the worries appear again. I have no money. Nobody wants to hear my message. Was it really God's guidance? Then comes the comforting assurance of last night. God has promised to take care of His honor, and in time I will be thankful for these days.

What a joy that God never leaves His children alone. He is a faithful guide for everyone who listens to His voice. "The LORD taketh pleasure . . . in those that hope in His mercy" (Psalm 147:11).

That day a Dutch service is held in a New York church. Dr. Barkay Wolf speaks, and many Hollanders meet afterwards for coffee in the vestry. The Reverend

Burggraaff, who baptized our Canadian-born princess, is presented to me. The name, ten Boom, revives a memory.

"I often tell the story of a nurse by that name," he says, "who experienced a miracle in a concentration camp with a bottle of vitamins. I tell it to prove that God still performs miracles as in Bible times. Do you happen to know that nurse? Is she related to you?"

"She is not a nurse," I reply, "but a watchmaker. It was I who had that experience in 1944."*

"Then you must come with me to Staten Island and tell my congregation of your experiences."

Together we go to the pleasant parsonage, where I spend five delightful days with those happy Christians and their two sweet children.

Mrs. Burggraaff is an excellent cook. I have been trying to discover how long one can exist on Nedick's ten-cent breakfasts: a large cup of coffee, two doughnuts, and a glass of orange juice, eaten while standing at a counter. The delicious nourishing food is a joy, but the real reason for my happiness is that I have ended my lesson in obedience and feel that God is at work opening doors and hearts.

Returning to New York, I see on a church door an invitation to attend the Lord's Supper. What a blessing lies in Holy Communion. As truly as I taste the bread and wine, the Lord's body was broken for me, and His blood shed for me. How I had missed the sacrament while in prison. On Sunday morning I shall go to that church. It will be Easter Sunday.

The churches of America have a friendly welcome for strangers. The minister greets me and gives me the

*A Prisoner and Yet . . . , 97.

address of Irving Harris, the editor of *The Evangel,* a monthly magazine distributed throughout America and many other lands. The next day I am telling him about my problems.

"I know I am walking in the way God has led me, but so many declare that there is no such thing as direct guidance."

"Pay no attention to the counsel of those who do not believe in guidance," he answers. "The Bible contains many promises that God will lead those who obey Him. 'Call unto Me, and I will answer thee' (Jeremiah 33:3). Have you ever heard of a Good Shepherd that did not lead his sheep?"

I am content. I know he is right.

"Do you have any copy that would be useful for my magazine?" he asks.

I give him a copy of my lectures and tell him to use as much as he can.

"There is one drawback," he explains. "We cannot pay. This paper exists only to spread the gospel, not for financial profit."

Wonderful! I am in the presence of an American who sees money in its proper perspective. "Seek ye first the kingdom of God, and His righteousness; and all these things shall be added unto you" (Matthew 6:33).

Mr. Harris gives me an address in Washington. Does it mean I am being fobbed off again? No, I have found a true friend, and with this recommendation Abraham Vereide receives me as a friend into his home. He invites me to dinner. Three other guests are present, professors who ask difficult questions. I feel like a schoolgirl invited out by her headmistress. My English is not very fluent, and my mistakes seem more glaring than ever before. But

I do my utmost to use my eyes and ears. I can learn much here listening to the conversation. I hear a good illustration. Mr. Vereide speaks about our relationship with Jesus and shows a train ticket. Printed on it are the words "Not good if detached."

From now on I choose that phrase as my slogan. Connected with Jesus, His victory is my victory. "Not good if detached from Him."

That afternoon I am asked to address a group of women. Whenever I am asked to witness to what the Lord meant to me during my imprisonment I am in my element. I can tell that Jesus Christ is a reality, even in darkest days. He is the answer to all the problems in the hearts of men and nations. It is evident that the Holy Spirit is at work in this meeting. There is response from these women who gather once a week for prayer and Bible study.

That evening one of them gives me a check that enables me to return all the money I borrowed in New York.

Now the tables are turned. Instead of no work, I must guard against overwork. Ten months in America, in many villages and towns. Ten months of carrying the gospel to churches, prisons, universities, schools, and clubs.

Then the pillar of fire and the cloud lead to Germany. The one land in the world where I do not want to go.

F. B. Meyer says, "God does not fill with His Holy Spirit those who believe in the fulness of the Spirit, or those who desire Him, but those who obey Him."

When I left the German concentration camp I said, "I'll go anywhere God sends me, but I hope never to Germany." Though I was unaware of it, that was disobedience.

In America there comes a time when guidance no longer seems to be given. When I pray no answer comes. I realize that the trouble is not with the Good Shepherd but with the sheep, and I ask, "Lord, am I disobeying you in some way?"

The answer comes clearly: "Germany."

A struggle follows, but victory soon comes, and I am able to say, "Yes, Lord, to Germany also."

3

Return to Germany

The time is short,
Too short toward any living
To cherish enmity.
Lay it aside
For His dear sake, forgiving
As He forgiveth thee.

Author Unknown

At a meeting in a friend's home I see a woman who does not look into my eyes. On asking my hostess who she is I am told that she is one of the nurses from the concentration camp, Ravensbrück. Suddenly I recognize her. Ten years ago I had to take my sister Betsie to the hospital barracks in the concentration camp where we were prisoners. Her feet were paralyzed. She was dying. This nurse was cruel to her and scolded her. At that moment of recognition hatred comes into my heart. I thought I had overcome it, but now I see her again, after all these years, and great bitterness is in my heart. For ten years I have harbored this hatred. Oh, the shame of it!

When I bring my sins to the Lord Jesus He casts them into the depths of the sea—forgiven and forgotten. He also puts up a sign: "NO FISHING ALLOWED!"

And I? Ten years, and I have neither forgiven nor forgotten what this woman did.

Ashamed, I confess my guilt. "Forgive me for my hatred, O Lord. Teach me to love my enemies."

What a joy that there is forgiveness and salvation from sin. The blood of Jesus Christ cleanses us from all sins if we confess them. It has never cleansed excuses. Instead of hatred, love enters my heart. After the meeting I try to speak with her, but she is unwilling to talk.

The next day I think of her and pray for her. I believe in the power of praying together. Jesus has said, "Where two or three are gathered together in My name, there am I in the midst of them." Not "I come," but "I am." Jesus is there first. He invites the two and threes to come. That is why I ask my hostess if she will pray with me. Then she tells me that a group of young girls have been praying for the nurse and for her salvation for several months.

That gives me courage. When people pray for the salvation of someone it indicates that God is working. He puts it in our hearts and minds to intercede; and what God begins, He will complete.

I find the address of the hospital where the nurse works and call her by telephone. I tell her that I have a meeting that night and would be very happy if she would come.

Amazed, she asks, "What? Do *you* want *me* to come?"

"Yes, that is why I called you."

"Then I'll come."

The whole evening she listens and looks straight into my eyes. I know that she listens with her heart. After the meeting I read with her from the Bible the way of salvation. First John 4:9 clinches the matter: "In this was manifested the love of God toward us, because that God sent

His only begotten Son into the world, that we might live through Him." She makes the decision that causes the angels to rejoice. Not only has my hatred gone, but I can love her. And I, who have kept in my subconsciousness feelings of hatred, the Lord now uses as a window through which His light can shine into her dark heart: His channel for streams of living water. What miraculous power there is in the blood of Jesus! He forgives, cleanses, and then makes us His instrument. He cleanses the earthen vessel that contains the treasure. Sinners, saved sinners, He uses as His ambassadors. What wonderful grace!

The Wrong Address

A sick woman sits in a dirty, messy little kitchen. There is hardly room for my stool. I am eager for a quiet talk with her because she has twice called on a fortune-teller who claimed magic healing power. I tell her what a great sin this is in God's sight, because it really means that we run away from God and ask the devil for help. That is why God calls this sin an abomination (Deuteronomy 18:10–12).

A great compassion comes into my heart for this woman. I tell her about the longing father-heart of God who loves us so much and who brought us in contact with an ocean of love through Jesus Christ. That is why God thinks it so terrible when we seek help from the enemy.

I notice that she is now listening differently. When I warned her earnestly she defended herself and resisted. Now I tell her with joy about that great love of God. She listens intently. I read to her what Jesus says: "Come unto Me, all ye that labour and are heavy laden, and I will give you rest" (Matthew 11:28). Before I leave she prays. She asks forgiveness for going to the fortune-teller, and then she praises and thanks God for the great riches she has in Jesus Christ.

Battle against Powers of Darkness

In Germany many people turn to the sin of sorcery and witchcraft. Is this true in other lands, I wonder? Many who talk with me complain of a darkness in their hearts that cannot be lifted, or ever-recurring thoughts of suicide. When I ask if they have called upon a fortune-teller they reply that they have, but they do not really believe in her power.

In the days of uncertainty when Germans in captivity were unable to send messages home, wives and mothers yearned to know the fate of their loved ones. Many visited fortune-tellers. Whether or not they got answers I do not know, but it is evident that the powers of darkness entered their hearts. They do not seem to know that this is sin.

Whether this is done out of curiosity or "just for fun," it gives entrance to demonic powers. So whenever I have a full week of meetings, one evening is reserved for proving from the Bible the sin of this practice. The wearing of amulets and charms and the foretelling of events by cards and horoscopes are all an abomination in God's sight. Deuteronomy 18:10–12 warns us, "There shall not be found among you any one that maketh his son or his daughter to pass through the fire, or that useth divination, or an observer of times, or an enchanter, or a witch, or a charmer, or a consulter with familiar spirits, or a wizard, or a necromancer. For all that do these things are an abomination unto the LORD: and because of these abominations the LORD thy God doth drive them out from before thee."

It is wonderful to have an answer also to this problem. Jesus came to overcome the works of Satan. The Bible says, "They overcame him [Satan] by the blood of the Lamb, and by the word of their testimony" (Revelation 12:11). Ours is the victory through the blood of the Lamb and the testimony of our witness.

Those that are with us are greater than those that are against us. We need not remain in the dark. Jesus said, "I am the Light of the world: he that followeth Me shall not walk in darkness, but shall have the light of life" (John 8:12). We possess the authority of His name.

How great a joy it is to bring the Good News of Jesus' victory into this darkness. But whenever I give this message I am so tired I can hardly reach my bed. My heart beats irregularly, and I feel that I am not at all well.

One evening I have a long talk with my heavenly Father. "I cannot continue like this, dear Lord. Why must I testify against this particular sin? So many of your faithful servants never mention it. I can't go on like this much longer and live. Perhaps another month or two, and then my heart will give out."

Then in the *Losungsbuch,* a book of daily readings in German, I read, "Be not afraid, but speak, and hold not thy peace: For I am with thee, and no man shall set on thee to hurt thee" (Acts 18:9–10). A short poem follows:

Though all the powers of hell attack,
Fear not, Jesus is Victor.

Joy fills my heart; this is God's answer. I pray, "Lord, I will obey, I will not fear and be silent. But with my hands on this promise I ask You to protect me with Your blood, that the demons cannot touch me."

At that moment something happens to my heart; it beats regularly. I know I am healed. After this when having spoken against sorcery and witchcraft, I feel as well as ever before. Jesus is Victor! The fear of demons comes from the demons themselves. We have nothing to be afraid of. Those who are with us are greater than those who are against us. Hidden with Christ in God: What a refuge! The mighty High Priest and His legions of angels are on our side.

Resist the Devil—Ours Is the Victory

In a small town in Germany a group of students plan a weekend. Ten Christians have each brought an outsider. Though the only speaker, I feel we are a team, these ten and I. There is much prayer and discussion between meetings, and when Sunday evening comes eight students have accepted Jesus as their personal Savior.

Trudy, a medical student, follows me that evening as, tired but grateful, I go to my room. "Corrie, thank you so much for all you have done for Heinz. He is my fiancé, and he is so different today. Before he was all gloom; now he is truly happy."

"What a joy, Trudy. Let us thank the Lord, for He has done it. I am only a branch of the Vine, a channel for His blessing. But tell me, Trudy, what about yourself?"

"I haven't come to speak about myself; I wish only to speak of Heinz."

"All right. Then we speak about the change in Heinz,

who has come out of darkness into God's marvelous light."

Suddenly I turn to Trudy and address the demons within her. In Jesus' name I bid them leave and go back to hell, where they belong. I see immediately a great change in Trudy's face. Astounded, she asks, "Is there hope for me?" Then she falls to her knees and cries, "I am free. Thank You, Lord, I am free!"

With deep joy Trudy praises the Lord, then confesses she contemplated committing suicide the next day. Looking into her eyes, I see she is not entirely free, but she leaves my room praising the Lord. My legs are trembling. I had known nothing about the girl, and all this seems to have happened outside of myself. What a victory! Though it is late, I go downstairs to find someone to join me in prayer. In the meeting room I find all the students on their knees.

"I've come to tell you that Trudy is free."

"Yes, we know."

"What do you know? Who told you?"

"We know she was under the influence of demons. When we saw her go to your room we all knelt in prayer and asked God to use you to deliver her. Suddenly our prayer became praise, and we knew she was free."

"She is not entirely free. Keep on praying for her until she is completely liberated."

Three days later I speak at the University that Trudy attends, but she hides behind others. The boys ask me to speak to her, but I have no guidance. A week later she looks me up in a town where I am working, and God uses me to finish the work He began in her.

I am well aware I do not possess the special gift to cast out demons, but in times of emergency we must dare to lay hold on the promise of Mark 16:17: "In My name shall they cast out devils."

More Than Psychology

Psychology is profitable, even necessary, but not enough. I recall a conversation with a German pastor. It had been a busy and difficult counseling session. Six people had complained about great inner darkness and thoughts of suicide. Some I had been able to help, but not all.

"Can't you help me?" I asked the pastor. "In cases like these working together is so much better. One can pray while the other casts out demons."

The pastor answered me with a discourse on the defense-mechanism of the subconscious. That was no help to me. How dangerous to try to solve great problems with small answers.

A theological professor was asked, "Do you teach your students to cast out demons?"

"Hardly," was the answer. "I can't do that myself."

"But you dare to send students to congregations that are filled with sorcery? Do you think their knowledge of the Jahist and the Elohist manuscripts of Genesis will help them when they are struggling with the demons that have entered so many people of our day?"

> Soldiers of Christ, arise,
> And put your armor on,
> Strong in the strength which God supplies
> Through His eternal Son;
> Strong in the Lord of hosts,
> And in His mighty power,
> Who in the strength of Jesus trusts

Is more than conqueror.
Leave no unguarded place,
No weakness of the soul;
Take every virtue, every grace,
And fortify the whole.
From strength to strength go on,
Wrestle and fight and pray,
Tread all the powers of darkness down
And win the well-fought day.

Charles Wesley

God's Love Never Fails

Once Betsie, my sister, and I walked through the color-less streets of a concentration camp.

"Corrie, these barracks here are used to destroy lives. We must pray God to give us such a camp after the war to build up lives."

What fantasy to see such possibilities in so terrible a place! No, it was not fantasy: It was faith. Faith sees the invisible, just as the radar of a ship throws its beam straight through the fog to the other ships. So faith shows God's love and Jesus' victory, even through the chaos of our life.

Many years later I walk again through the streets of a concentration camp. The war is over, but left behind are many wounds for many nations; perhaps the most serious wounds in Germany itself. In many countries there are refugees, homeless people, but here the problem seems almost beyond solution. No use trying to solve it—but no, we must not say that. Everyone must do what he can. God gave me a concentration camp. It was in Darmstadt, where shortly after the war I found several of my former guards. They were then prisoners; I was free. They had been very cruel. How their experiences during the war had demoralized them. Young women still, now imprisoned behind barbed wire; but more imprisoned by demonic powers. I could speak to them of Jesus' victory, His love for sinners, and His finished work on the cross when He carried the sins of the whole world, theirs included.

When I returned to the camp it was empty. The women had been freed or sent to other prisons. The same week I rented the whole camp, and now it is a place where refugees can stay while they build houses in the neighborhood.

When in Germany I visit the camp. I look around me. The barracks are grey, the streets between colorless. I tell Walter Zipf, the director, that it still looks like a prison camp. We make plans, and that very week God gives me enough money to enable us to fulfill them.

What a change bright green paint and flowers, many flowers, can make to a place! Two months later I receive a colored photograph, and now, with a little bit of imagination, it is more like a Hollywood home than a prison camp.

Human love has failed in this world, but the love of God is shed abroad in our hearts by the Holy Spirit who is given to us (Romans 5:5). It is this love that overcomes and is able to change even a colorless prison camp into a garden of flowers.

A Minister's Meeting

Working in Germany is a delight. The ministers and I get along well, working, praying, and striving together. A team traveling with me would be ideal, but since that is not yet possible, God has given me as teammates the ministers in whose churches I work. Though differing in background and training, our common aim unites us: the winning of souls for eternity and helping the children of God to learn that "Jesus is Victor."

Speaking at a ministers' meeting is another story. Frequently it is among them that I find my severest critics, and sometimes even my greatest opposition. Yet it seems vital to be used of God among them, for these men who work in over-large congregations and are weighed down with problems also need to be reminded of Jesus' victory and His plan for the world.

A large group waits for me to speak. Shall I try to convince them *not* to listen to me but to God and His message for us?

"Gentlemen, I am a layperson, a laywoman, a Dutch laywoman. Are there some present who would rather not remain?

"I intend to speak about conversion. Perhaps you have a label for me . . . a pietist? I shall speak about the Lord's return: That should label me a sectarian. I may even speak about the rapture of the church: That makes me a fanatic; of the fulness of the Holy Spirit: a Pentecostal. Keep your labels handy, gentlemen. Should my words touch your consciences, you have only to label me, set me in a corner, and have nothing to fear."

A strange thing happens. The critical faces relax. There is laughter, after which we truly listen together to God's message: Germany's great need, and Christ the answer to this need. The world's history is a great embroidery by God, enough of which is made clear to us through His Word so that we can face the future calm and secure, since all is in His hand. Indeed, the best is yet to be—a world full of the knowledge of the Lord, as the waters cover the sea.

When I finish, with one accord the group turns to prayer.

Carl

"Behold I saw an ocean of light and love flow over an ocean of darkness and death, and in that I saw the infinite love of God, and the day it flowed over the ocean of darkness and death was when Jesus said, 'It is finished!'" (Wesley).

Everywhere in Germany I find the wounds and scars of war. I read a letter a mother has received from her son, Carl, now a prisoner in the Netherlands. He was a prison guard during the war and has been sentenced to sixteen years' imprisonment in the very jail where he had practiced his cruelties. He writes, "Father, Mother, I have accepted the Lord Jesus as my Savior. He has made me a child of God. I have brought all my sins to Him and He has cast them into the depths of the sea."

After reading that letter I decide to request an amnesty for him from my Queen. A child of God has power in his struggle against Satan. He has the authority of Jesus' name. Even as a traffic policeman is backed by the authority of the law, and traffic stops at his signal, so too, Satan has to yield to the name of Jesus. Every child of God can wield the authority of the name that is above every other name. That is why I can trust Carl.

Before I write the letter to the Queen I decide to go to Vught to call on Carl. Again I see that courtyard where Betsie and I stood, not knowing what was in store for us. We stood between rows of men who told us we might well be shot. I tremble as I see this spot once more. Then I enter the cell occupied by Carl, my former prison guard.

"I come to bring you greetings from your parents, Carl."

"Do you mean to say you have seen them?"

"Certainly; I've just returned from Germany."

Carl's eyes fill with tears, and he whispers, "How is Mother?"

"She's well, Carl, and so happy you have decided for Jesus and are now a child of God." I describe my visit to his parents and friends, and then add, "I, too, was in prison here."

"You were? When?"

"In 1944."

Carl's face turns pale. "Then we know each other."

"Yes, we know each other."

In memory we both recall Carl's cruelties of those days, but a joyful look lights his face as he says, "How happy I am that my sins have been taken away."

I say nothing, but a dark thought wells up in my soul: Is it as easy as that? Due to your barbarism and the cruelties of others, my father, Betsie, Kik, my cousin, and many of my friends perished in prisons and concentration camps. But you are no longer guilty!

It is an immutable law of God that man finds peace only when he is continually ready to forgive. Suddenly I see what I am doing. Carl's sins have been cast by Jesus into the depths of the sea. They are forgiven and forgotten —and I am trying to fish them up again! I pray, "Father, in Jesus' name forgive these thoughts. Lord Jesus, keep me close to You as the branch is close to the vine, that I may be able to forgive and forget, and love my enemies."

Only now do I trust myself to speak again. "Indeed,

Carl, your sins have been taken away. Our Lord has taken upon Himself the sins of the whole world, including yours and mine. I have something more to tell you. I am planning to write to the Queen to ask an amnesty for you."

A lesson is learned there in Carl's cell. When Jesus requires that we love our enemies, He gives us the love He demands from us. We are channels of His love, not reservoirs. Truly, if I had been a reservoir, at that moment it would have sprung a great leak and all the love would have drained away. Again my American railway ticket gives the answer, "Not good if detached." That is me! I have been detached. But when I am united with Him who prayed on the cross, "Father, forgive them; for they know not what they do," I can forgive and forget, and even love my enemies. Without Him I am embittered and am prone to hate. Therefore I want ever to remain close to Him, as the branch is to the vine, "That My joy might remain in you, and that your joy might be full" (John 15:11). Once we learn to love our enemies we tap the ocean of God's love as never before.

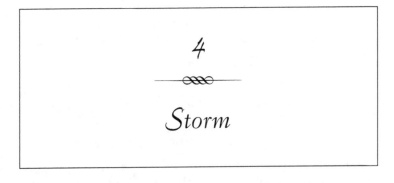

4

Storm

As the branch cannot bear fruit of itself, except it abide in the vine; no more can ye, except ye abide in me.

John 15:4

It is so tiring to hold the edge of my bed during the rolling of the ship that I fasten myself with a rope to my mattress. I am the only passenger on board the freighter, and I must share my cabin with the gyrocompass. I am a bad sailor and find sea travel a tribulation. Suddenly a huge wave hurls against the ship and I hear a strange sound. The gyrocompass whistles night and day, but now it is broken and the noise is peculiar. One of the engineers comes to repair it.

"Is this a bad storm?" I ask.

"Why, no! This is nothing at all. Wait until the wind force is fourteen, then we shall really know what rolling is."

At that moment, as if to contradict his words, a big wave throws the ship to one side. I hear the breaking of china, and everything that is not securely fastened runs from one side of the cabin to the other.

The storm has subsided by next morning, so I climb up to the bridge and meet the captain. After a chat about the weather, I say, "Captain, it is Sunday. May we have a church service?"

"What? A church service on my ship? It would be the first in my life!"

"Then," I reply with a smile, "it is high time you began, sir."

"All right. You can use the mess room. I am not opposed to the idea."

He himself writes on the notice board that at 11:00 A.M. there will be a church service in the mess room. At the appointed time nobody appears. The cabin boy brings me a cup of coffee. It is a Dutch ship, and the ship's cook knows that at 11:00 A.M. a cup of coffee is a tradition.

"Are you going to stay?" I ask the boy. "I have a very interesting story to tell you."

"I don't want to hear that nonsense," he says. "I will not have anything to do with that Bible and God business." He feels very cocksure and leaves me alone.

I never saw so empty a church; just a cup of coffee and myself. I am not at all on fire for the Lord. Were I enthusiastic, I would go to the bridge and say, "Come along, gentlemen; you must help me to fill the mess room. Send your men and boys." But I don't do that. I go to my cabin and am very seasick. That is the only thing I can do during the whole week.

Sunday comes round again. I am feeling discouraged and ashamed. "Lord, I have now been on this ship for almost ten days, and I have done nothing to bring the gospel to all these men who may lose their souls for eternity. Lord, I am not a missionary. Send me back to my watchmaking business. I am not worthy to do your work."

At that moment I find in my Bible a little piece of paper that I have never seen before. On it is written:

Cowardly, wayward, and weak,
I change with the changing sky,
Today so eager and strong,
Tomorrow not caring to try.
But He never gives in,
And we two shall win,
    Jesus and I.

Instantly I see it! Indeed I am not worthy at all. The branch without the Vine cannot produce fruit, but I can do all things through Christ who gives me strength. The strongest and the weakest branches are worth nothing without the Vine, but connected to it they have the same nature.

I go up to the bridge. "Captain, it is Sunday. Can we have a church service?"

"Again? In a church as empty as last week?" he asks teasingly.

"No, Captain. Not empty, but full, and you must help me."

He does, and there are ten men in the mess room. When my sermon is finished the cabin boy says, "It was not boring at all!"

5

Ambassadors for Christ

Make me a match that can kindle a fire.

Bermuda, island of wealth and bright colors, deep-blue sea, white-walled houses, and an abundance of flowers.

Bermuda, land of ever-smiling sunshine.

But Bermuda also has prisons. I speak in one soon after my arrival. While I tell of God's great love in Jesus Christ and the riches that abide in any circumstance if we "cash our checks," that is, act on His Word, God touches the heart of the prison director.

"Please come again," he says. "You speak a language the prisoners understand."

I am eager to return. "How often may I come?"

"As often as you wish."

"Twice a day?" When I am offered a finger I take the whole hand. Such opportunities are rare. Usually one chance to speak is all that is permitted in prisons. Then one often leaves with a heavy heart. How one would like to delve deeper into the prisoners' problems and draw more generously from the bottomless ocean of the riches of Christ's love.

But here this splendid offer. "Agreed. Twice a day."

Arrangements are made for a meeting with the assembled prisoners each morning, and an hour is spent in the evening going from cell to cell. Cell doors are barred with heavy iron grills. Standing outside, I read the Scriptures to the inmates. The attendant, a Negro of great understanding, takes me to a man who desperately needs an encouraging word, or to another who has requested an interview. He shows much tact, for he withdraws and remains at a distance till I give a sign that I am ready to go.

In one cell there are two Negroes. One keeps himself in the background while the other tells me his troubles, his hands tensed around the bars of his cell. What a joy! How glorious that with the utmost conviction I can tell him that the Lord Jesus carried the sins of the whole world, that He finished this task for him too. From my spiritual "first-aid kit" I read some verses to show the way of salvation. Witnessing and telling of my own experiences may be important, but the Word of God is the "sharp two-edged sword."

Even while speaking I am in constant prayer. Both the vertical and the horizontal contacts are necessary. After all, it is not I who am at work but the Holy Spirit working through me as a channel, a branch of the Vine. I pray that God may remove all the man's "ifs" and "buts" that the way from darkness to God's marvelous light may be opened. Finally, he says, "Yes, Lord Jesus."

Nothing more? No, not yet. But it means that he has accepted the Lord as his Savior and is now a child of God (John 1:12), that he has opened the door of his heart to Him who stands outside and knocks, and now promises to come and abide with him (Revelation 3:20).

"Do you know how to pray?" I ask the Negro crouched in a corner of the cell.

"Oh, yes."

"Then please come here."

He comes, and I ask him to clasp the hand of his cell-mate while I take his other hand and the hand of the man who has just decided for Jesus. A tiny prayer circle reaching through the bars of a prison door.

"Will you pray first?"

"Our Father which art in heaven, hallowed be Thy name . . ."

Suddenly silence descends upon the corridor as the other Negro prisoners standing behind their doors hear one of their number pray.

"Thy kingdom come. Thy will be done on earth, as it is in heaven."

Are the others praying with us? Are their minds on that future when God's will shall be done on earth as it is in heaven? No more prisons there. The earth full of the knowledge of the Lord as the waters cover the sea.

"Give us this day our daily bread, and forgive us our trespasses, as we forgive them that trespass against us." Forgiveness—no longer guilty, but mercifully pardoned.

"And lead us not into temptation, but deliver us from evil." The possibility of victory in the midst of evil.

"For Thine is the kingdom, and the power, and the glory, for ever and ever. Amen."

Prisoners speak to a King! Weak ones, poor ones, praying and giving thanks for power and glory. It is a sacred moment in the Bermuda prison. Have the demons left because angels are present? Jesus Himself is present. "Where two or three are gathered together in My name, there am I in the midst of them," He has said. There is joy among the angels over one sinner that is saved.

The sinner himself now prays. It is a poor little prayer;

his first. Though stammering and stumbling, it is the thanks of one who for the first time has seen the marvelous light of God's love in Jesus Christ. It means, "Thank You, Lord Jesus, because You have saved me and will keep on saving me." Do I see tears in the eyes of the attendant as he takes me to another corridor?

In a cell corner I see a crouching figure, a red patch on the back of his prison uniform.

"Has he tried to escape?" I ask the attendant.

"Yes, but how did you know?"

"We also had to wear red patches if we tried to escape from prison."

"This is a tragic case. The man, a murderer, was sentenced to be flogged. He feared the beating so much that he tried to run away. Now he has had to bear double punishment."

Poor man! I pray, "Lord, help me to find the way to reach this man's heart."

Suddenly my own prison experiences come to my mind. When our fellow-prisoners were tortured we urged them to tell us all that had happened. It was hard listening, but it helped them to throw off their terrible experience. If it is possible to get this man to talk, perhaps I can find the way to his heart.

"Hello! Did you have a beating?" I ask.

"Yes."

"Was it bad?"

"Yes."

"Come, tell me. Did they take you to the hospital afterwards?"

"No, it wasn't that bad." He comes to the barred door and looks at me with wondering eyes. What kind of a woman is this who asks such questions?

And my heart says, "Thank you, God; he is already at the door!"

"Didn't they do anything for you?"

"Yes, they rubbed me with salve."

Then I inquire, "Is there hate in your heart?"

"Hate! I am full of hate."

"That is something I can understand."

"*You . . . ?*"

"Certainly. I know how you feel." Then I tell him of the beatings I had in Ravensbrück and, even worse, the beatings given to my poor weak sister Betsie because she no longer had the strength to shovel dirt. Then hatred tried to enter into my heart, but a miracle happened, for Jesus filled my heart with God's love, and there was no room for hatred.

Then I say, "If you will accept Him as your Savior, He will do the same for you."

I take my Bible and read, "'As many as received Him, to them gave He power to become the sons of God' (John 1:12). Jesus is knocking at the door of your heart. If you will let Him, He will come in (Revelation 3:20)."

It is a struggle between life and death, but life wins. He, too, utters his yes to Jesus, and the angels in heaven rejoice. We pray together, and he also offers a stammering prayer. Then we shake hands through the bars.

"Ah, miss, just a moment. Have you a little more time?"

"Certainly. Why?"

"Across the hall in the third cell is a man in real trouble. Won't you tell him this same story of Jesus?'

A babe in Christ, not more than five minutes saved, and already he has a burden for souls. Only just saved himself, and he longs to share his joy with others.

So often people say, "I don't know enough myself. I'm too young in the faith to point out the way to others." Then I always ask, "How old a babe in Christ was the Samaritan woman when she declared to the entire city, 'Come, see a man, which told me all things that ever I did. Is not this the Christ?'" Many went to Jesus, and later said to her, "Now we believe, not because of thy saying, for we have heard Him ourselves." A babe in Christ for only half an hour and already a wholesale soul winner!

I go to the cell across the hall and have a long talk with the inmate. At last he understands what Jesus meant when He said, "Him that cometh to Me I will in no wise cast out." And he, too, accepts the Lord Jesus.

Before I leave the prison I go back to the murderer and tell him, "That was a wonderful thing you did when you sent me to the man across the hall. He, too, made a decision for Jesus." Then the Negro looks past me and cries, "Hi, brother!"

I think in that moment of a little poem:

When I enter that beautiful city,
And the saved all around me appear,
I hope that someone will tell me,
"It was you who invited me here."

What a joy when we reach heaven to hear someone say, "Hi, brother! Hi, sister! You invited me here." Then indeed we shall know we have not lived in vain. Not hay, not stubble, but silver and gold have we built on the one foundation, Jesus Christ (1 Corinthians 3:10–16).

Sometimes I am asked, "Can people really be saved so quickly?"

I always answer, "How long did it take Levi, the tax

collector? Jesus said, 'Follow me,' and he promptly closed his office and followed the Lord."

"Yes, but that was Jesus."

"Who do you suppose it was in the Bermuda prison? Do you think it was Corrie ten Boom who converted that man? No, it was Jesus who has said, 'Verily, verily, I say unto you, He that believeth on Me, the works that I do shall he do also; and greater works than these shall he do; because I go unto My Father' (John 14:12)."

Jesus is at the right hand of God the Father and does even greater things than He did during the three and a half years He taught in Palestine. But He works through His church, you and me and all those who are united with Him, the branches of the Vine that bring forth good fruit.

"God, who first ordered light to shine in darkness, has flooded our hearts with His light. We now can enlighten men only because we can give them knowledge of the glory of God, as we see it in the face of Jesus Christ. This priceless treasure we hold, so to speak, in a common earthenware jar—to show that the splendid power of it belongs to God and not to us" (2 Corinthians 4:6–7 PHILLIPS). Streams of living water shall flow from us if we go through life united with Him.

6

---

*L*oneliness

God has plans—no problems. There is no panic in heaven.

Ian Thomas

Living in an isolated house in Canada is a woman who needs my help. It takes me a couple of hours to get there. When I arrive she is sitting in her chair, one arm on the table. She stares through the window at the wide prairie, which seems to be endless. Conversation is difficult, and during the moments when we are not talking the depressing silence in and around the house bears in on me.

I open the Bible and begin to read, "'Yea, though I walk through the valley of the shadow of death, I will fear no evil: for Thou art with me" (Psalm 23:4). "Who shall separate us from the love of Christ? Shall tribulation, or depression, or loneliness? No, in all these things we are more than conquerors through Him that loved us'" (Romans 8:35).

Then she begins to talk, at first slowly and hesitantly —then with greater confidence she describes the big city in Europe where she grew up. Then her marriage and subsequent emigration with her husband to Canada.

"I have five children. One of them is married; the others all work here on the ranch. They will come back tonight at six o'clock, and supper must be ready for them. When they are all at home it is not quiet here any more. At first we had our own farm where it was never quiet, for everyone in the family was always working in and around the house. But now they work for other farmers. We have had difficulties and setbacks—storms, drought, cattle sickness, and locust. Then we came here, where it is so quiet and lonely."

When she finishes speaking she seems to be a little less unhappy. I can pray with her, and I know that she listens. Does she pray? When I get up to go she comes with me to the door. From the car, as I drive off, I can see her standing there. Is it the setting sun that brings a little color to her cheeks? She waves to me and calls out, "Thank you." Will I ever hear of her again?

Yes, I do hear of her. A letter comes when I am alone in my cheerless hotel room in the big city. My windows look onto a small inner square; there is no sun and almost no light. I open the letter. "Corrie, the evening after your visit, the woman killed her daughter with a gun. She is now in an asylum."

Is the devil victor? Poor woman. Poor family.

A great darkness enters my heart. What suffering there is in the world. This is only a drop in the ocean of misery on this earth. Have I failed? Have I done wrong? I do not often weep, but now I cannot restrain the tears. Then I take the Book that always gives comfort. "Cast thy burden upon the Lord." Yes, I need not carry it myself. He has carried our sorrows. I unpack my mental suitcase in prayer and pray for grace to travel farther with it empty and to leave my sorrows with Him. Then I read further,

"Behold, I make all things new," says Jesus (Revelation 21:5). "The earth shall be full of the knowledge of the LORD" (Isaiah 11:9). "God shall wipe away all tears from their eyes" (Revelation 21:4).

I pray, "Lord Jesus, come quickly. It is so dark in the world." Then I read the psalms written by people in darkness and in the depths of misery but who had found the answer by God's Spirit. "Hide not Thy face far from me. . . . Thou hast been my help; leave me not, neither forsake me, O God of my salvation. . . . Wait on the LORD: be of good courage, and He shall strengthen thine heart: wait, I say, on the LORD" (Psalm 27:9, 14).

I do not understand it yet, but trustingly I put my hand in His hand, like a sad child who knows his father does not make mistakes.

I read another letter. A friend writes, "In Mexico, an automobile accident occurred. A missionary with four of his children and seven promising students of a Bible school were killed."

In Mexico, where the fields are already white unto harvest and the laborers are few. What is the reason for it, Lord? I do not understand it. There seems no answer at all. One day we will understand. "At present we are men looking at puzzling reflections in a mirror. The time will come when we shall see reality whole and face to face! At present all I know is a little fraction of the truth, but the time will come when I shall know it as fully as God now knows me" (1 Corinthians 13:12 PHILLIPS).

7

The Young Canadian

When Satan tempts me to despair
And tells me of my sins within;
Upwards I look and see Him there
Who made an end of all my sin.

I like the Canadians. Is it because they combine, more or less, that young, free attitude of the Americans with the traditions of Britain? In Victoria I have a talk with a businessman. In his beautiful car he takes me to a church where I am to speak that evening.

"Can you drive and pray at the same time?" I ask.

"Oh, yes. But we have time to park for five minutes. It is a good thing to pray before going to church."

After we have prayed, he leans against his steering wheel and tells me about himself.

"Years ago I accepted Jesus Christ as my Savior. I have read many books. I have studied my Bible during my quiet time and have listened to the best sermons it is possible to hear in Victoria. But there is absolutely no joy in me. Sometimes I try to help people, but very soon pass them on to others. In my heart there is bitterness instead of love. There is . . ."

"You remind me of a branch of the vine that says, 'I cannot understand why I bear no fruit.' It doesn't see that the whole question is whether or not it is in contact with the vine. Why not stop thinking of the fruit for a time and think only of the vine? Why have you no connection with the Lord Jesus?"

"My sins. I am bitter, selfish, and unkind. What can you do with your sins?"

"I always do what is written in 1 John 1:9: Confess my sins."

"But it doesn't help. I remain bitter and dark."

"Do you believe that the blood of Jesus cleanses from sins?'

"Sure I do."

"Where are the sins that you have confessed? What does the Bible say? Your bitterness is in the depths of the sea, forgiven and forgotten, and there is a little notice that says 'NO FISHING ALLOWED.' Your selfishness disappeared like that cloud we saw five minutes ago in the sky. Your unkindness is as far away from you as the east is from the west."

"But in a few minutes I am committing the same sins."

"When it is three o'clock and you are conscious of bitterness, confess it at three o'clock. You have an advocate with the Father—Jesus. He takes that sin on His own shoulders and cleanses you with His blood. When the devil comes three minutes later to accuse you, there is no bitterness left. Be sure that you come to the Father with your sin three minutes sooner than the accuser. You can then say, with your hand on the Bible, '[God] hath made Him to be sin for us, who knew no sin; that we might be made the righteousness of God in Him'

(2 Corinthians 5:21). When Jesus died on the cross He identified Himself with our death, and now you and I must identify ourselves with His life. So if the connection between the branch and the vine remains, the fruit comes from the vine. The branch does not help the vine. The vine does not help the branch. The vine does everything, and the branch must keep connected with it. That electric lamp there does not help the generator. The generator does not help the lamp. The generator gives all the power. The lamp must only be connected. You do not help the Holy Spirit. The Holy Spirit does not help you. The Holy Spirit does everything—the only condition is that you must keep in contact.

"It is such a joy to live by faith, simply acting on what the Bible says. Then Jesus' hand keeps hold of ours. Thank Him for that. In 1 Corinthians 15:57 it says, 'Thanks be to God, which giveth us the victory through our Lord Jesus Christ.'

"When the devil makes me depressed I always think of the immigrant and the peanuts. An immigrant and his family were on a big steamer. He had a bag full of peanuts; at every mealtime they all ate peanuts. Of course, this diet became very monotonous, and one day the immigrant asked the purser how much it would cost for his family and himself to have one of the meals that he could smell cooking so deliciously. The purser answered smilingly that they were permitted to enjoy every meal served, without cost, as they had already been paid for when the immigrant tendered his passage money. Don't you think that the man changed his diet from the peanuts to the good meals that were served on the big steamer?

"Jesus paid for everything when He died on the cross.

The handwriting of our sins is nailed on that cross. Turn away from your peanuts. Stop trying yourself and take the riches that are yours through Jesus Christ. You are what you are in Him. Live like a king's child, and not like a beggar. Norman Grubb says, 'Break through the bands of HAVE-NOT-LIFE.' When all demons and men tell me 'You have not,' then I declare, 'I have' because it is written.

"But don't forget to make right the wrong you have done. After you have asked forgiveness for unkindness, and you do not make it right with the person who has suffered through it, then you leave tools in the hands of the enemy. This restitution is given also through a branch connected with the Vine. A child of God connected with Jesus Christ is right with God, and right with men.

"After you have confessed your sins, claim the promise Jesus made about the Holy Spirit: 'I will send Him unto you' (John 16:7). The Holy Spirit is here: Jesus sent Him at Pentecost. Obey the joyful commandment, 'Be filled with the Spirit' (Ephesians 5:18), and then the fruit will come.

"What fruit does the Holy Spirit have? He has love, joy, peace, longsuffering, gentleness, goodness, faithfulness, meekness, and self-control. Jesus was all these when He was on earth. I once read somewhere 'The fruit of the Spirit is a perfect portraiture of Christ.'

"Love is the love of Christ that passes knowledge. Joy is the joy unspeakable and full of glory. Peace is the peace that passes all understanding that Jesus promised when He said, 'My peace I give unto you.' Longsuffering is forgiving—even your enemies, just as Jesus forgave His when He was on the cross. Gentleness is the reproduction of the gentleness of Jesus. Goodness is Christlikeness: a kindly disposition. The next fruit is faithfulness. The disciples were not always faithful. At the betrayal of Jesus in the garden, they all forsook Him and fled. But when the Holy Spirit came down at Pentecost they all became faithful unto death. Meekness—that is not the same as weakness. Nor is it a native fruit of the human heart. It is an exotic from heaven. Self-control means mastering the appetites and passions, particularly the sensual.

"All this fruit can be seen in you, but only when you are in contact with the Vine. You are 'not good if detached.'"

Although I have a different sermon prepared, I speak that evening about the Vine and the branch.

8

⚬⚬⚬

Memories from a Concentration Camp

Faith in Jesus Christ makes the uplook good, the outlook high, the inlook favorable, and the future glorious.

In thought I return to the years of my imprisonment. Because my friends and my family and I had housed and hidden Jews during the Nazi occupation we had been sent to the concentration camp in Ravensbrück. Fourteen hundred of us were packed in barracks built to house four hundred. It was unspeakably filthy. The vile blankets and thin mattresses on which we spent our days and nights were hosts to multitudes of vermin. Lice carried disease, rampant everywhere. But they performed one service for us; the Aufseherinnnen (women guards) and officers never honored the barracks with their presence. They had a healthy fear of our bugs. Therefore, though the Bible was strictly forbidden and dubbed a "Book of Lies," we could hold Bible studies twice a day in our barracks. God can use even vermin for His purposes.

Prisoners came to us from all directions and listened while we read and interpreted the Bible. Above and all around us, beds were closely stacked in triple tiers. There was respectful silence, and I know many were hearing the good news of God's great love through Jesus Christ for the first time in their lives.

A Hollander, Mrs. De Boer, approached me one evening. She seemed desperate, her eyes full of fear. "Corrie, can you help me? I am afraid. I've just seen a woman cruelly beaten to death. It was terrible! When will my time come to be killed? I am afraid of death. Do help me. Perhaps you can tell me something from your Book that will take away this terrible fear."

"Yes, indeed I can," I replied. "This Book has the answer in John 1:12: 'As many as received Him, to them gave He power to become the sons of God.' If you are a child of God you need not fear death, for in John 14:2 we read, 'In My Father's house are many mansions!' 'I,' Jesus said, 'go to prepare a place for you.' Children of God are at home in the Father's house. To them death is the gateway to heaven."

"That says nothing to me," answered Mrs. De Boer. "I'm not religious; I've never read the Bible; I don't attend church. When you say I must accept Jesus I simply don't know what you mean."

I prayed for wisdom. How can this mystery be made clear? How wonderful that we read in James 1:5, "If . . . any of you does not know how to meet any particular problem he has only to ask God—who gives generously to all men without making them feel foolish or guilty—and he may be quite sure that the necessary wisdom will be given him" (PHILLIPS).

"Do you recall years ago when Mr. De Boer proposed to you? How did you answer him?"

She smiled sadly and replied, "I said yes."

"Exactly. And when you had spoken that one little word you belonged to one another, you to him and he to you. Today Jesus asks, 'Will you accept Me as your Savior?' If you say, 'Yes, Lord,' then you belong to Him and He belongs to you."

"Is it as simple as that?" she asked.

"Yes. To become a child of God you need only to accept Him; salvation is a gift. Jesus says in Revelation 3:20, 'Behold, I stand at the door, and knock: if any man hear My voice, and open the door, I will come in to him.' Of course, that is only the beginning; there is more to follow. After you had accepted your fiancé, you sent announcements to tell your friends that you were engaged. When you accept the Lord Jesus you also tell others that you belong to Him.

"A very important day in your life was your wedding day. Then you were truly united for better or worse, in joy or in sorrow. When you take Jesus as your Savior you will step into a world of wealth, the wealth of this Book, the Bible. Then you can claim all of His promises. As you read this Book you will realize that you can be a free and happy child of God when you completely surrender your life to Him. You cast everything on Him: your sins, your cares, your all. Most wonderful of all is the fact that you must cast your sins upon Him. God is the only one in the whole wide world who can deal with the problem of our sins."

We sat quietly for a few moments, and then together we prayed. She, too, prayed and gave her answer to Jesus—"Yes." Nothing more? No, not for the moment, but when someone for the first time comes to Jesus with an honest yes, the angels in heaven rejoice over the soul that has been redeemed.

When I met her the next day she was truly happy and at peace. "I am well aware," she said, "that they can do anything they please with us, even cruelly murder us, but I know also that no one can take out of my heart the peace and happiness that I have found now that I know Jesus lives in my heart."

That same day I met her friend, Mrs. De Goede. "Why not take the same step your friend has taken?" I asked. "See how she has been changed. You, too, can have the same peace."

Her face hardened. "That's not for me. You know nothing of my past. I'm too wicked to be a Christian, one of those pious ones. Oh, no! Being a Christian is all very well for noble souls, but not for me. I'm far too wicked," she repeated.

"Just one moment," I said. "When you read your Bible you will notice there was only one kind of people the Lord could not help—the Pharisees. In their own eyes they were so perfect they needed no Savior. But sinners were never rejected by the Lord Jesus. To them he said, 'Him that cometh to Me I will in no wise cast out' (John 6:37).

"Do you know what the Bible tells us about sins we confess? God drowns them in the depths of the sea. As far as the east is from the west, He casts our sins from us. He throws them away behind Him. He makes them disappear like a cloud. You saw that cloud a moment ago? Now it has disappeared. Where is it? Completely gone! Thus Jesus causes our sins to disappear. John says, 'If we confess our sins, He is faithful and just to forgive us our sins, and to cleanse us from all unrighteousness' (1 John 1:9)."

Together we read the parable of the prodigal son, and she, too, made the decision for Christ; that decision so necessary for time and eternity, since it means that our names are written in the Book of Life.

It was a few months later that I was standing at the gate of Ravensbrück waiting to be released. When the gate opened I would be free. A friend came to bid me farewell. She took my hand and asked, "Have you heard that Mrs. De Boer and Mrs. De Goede both died today?" Deeply shocked, I gazed once more toward the cruel, bleak camp, and said, "Lord, I thank You that it was Your will to have me here, if only for the sake of those two. But I know You have used Betsie and me to lead many more to Yourself, and that is worth all our suffering, even Betsie's death."

Betsie, my sister, had died a week earlier, but to have been used to save souls for eternity is worth living and dying for.

And now I am in America, in Oak Harbor. Oak Harbor is situated in a remote corner of America, in the extreme northwest. We drive for hours in a car through beautiful country, and now I stand before a small group of people in a tiny church. I relate my experiences as a prisoner and also tell of the conversion of Mrs. De Boer and Mrs. De Goede. The latter's sister is present. She knew that her sister had died somewhere in prison, but it was my lot to cross the ocean and drive across America to an out-of-the-way place to tell her that her sister had been saved for eternity. So is God's way.

Later we sit together on her porch, and she is deeply stirred as she hears the story of her sister's suffering, but also the story of her glorious salvation; saved through Christ Jesus and translated into glory.

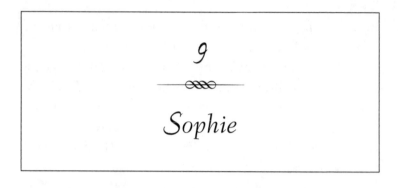

9

Sophie

Each redeemed heart is a vast reservoir of potential-
ity for God, laid up in store for the drinking of eternal
joys to come.

Mitchell

In a sanatorium in Norton a girl is dying. She has only a
small part of one lung left; an oxygen apparatus helps
her to breathe. It is a joy to be with her. In her room is the
free atmosphere that the approach of death can give
where people are ready to die. She is standing on the edge
of eternity, and it is as if we have a bird's-eye view of
earthly things; we see the reality, and earthly illusions go
to the background.

"Do you know, Corrie, it will be so joyful to work in
heaven. What do you think it will be like?"

"I don't know much, but I believe there will be
tremendous activity, without the impediments of this
world. We have to reign with Jesus over the world, and we
shall be so pure, so filled with God's Spirit, that we shall
have every ability to do the work according to His pattern.
Here, we have already got the victory through Jesus
Christ, but it is still a battle against sins. There will be an
absolute absence of sin in heaven."

"Do you believe that we go immediately to heaven after we die?"

"The Lord Jesus said to the murderer on the cross, 'Today shalt thou be with me in Paradise.' His body was still on the cross the same moment that he was with Jesus in Paradise. I believe that everyone who dies in Jesus immediately rises in Paradise. Paul was longing for that when he wrote, 'We are . . . willing rather to be absent from the body, and to be present with the Lord' (2 Corinthians 5:8). He also wrote about the coming of our Lord for His own, when our bodies will be resurrected. I think then the souls from Paradise will be connected with celestial bodies again, and together we will meet the Lord Jesus in the air."

"Corrie, I know that I have eternal life. 'These things have I written unto you that believe on the name of the Son of God; that ye may know that ye have eternal life' (1 John 5:13), but sometimes I am afraid when I think of the moment of dying. Even the deathbeds of children of God can be dark."

"Then pray now that the Lord Jesus will protect you in that moment from the dark powers. That is a prayer that will always be answered. Turn your eyes to the future. Samuel Rutherford wrote in the sixteenth century, 'Our little inch of time of suffering is not worthy of our first night's welcome home to Heaven.' Paul says, 'The sufferings of this present time are not worthy to be compared with the glory which shall be revealed in us' (Romans 8:18)."

"Corrie, read the beginning of John 14 again."

"Jesus said, 'Let not your heart be troubled: ye believe in God, believe also in Me. In My Father's house are many mansions: if it were not so, I would have told you.

I go to prepare a place for you.' Our citizenship is in heaven; we are heavenly citizens. Our home is there. Death is a tunnel. Moody once said, 'In the valley of the shadow of death there must be a light, otherwise there could not be shadow.' Jesus is our light. '[He] is able to keep you from falling,' says Jude in verse 24, 'and to present you before His glory without fault and with unspeakable joy' (PHILLIPS). When He holds us, He keeps us; when He keeps us, He guides us; when He guides us, He will one day bring us safely home. When His hand holds us we will not fear, even 'though the earth be removed, and though the mountains be carried into the midst of the sea' (Psalm 46:2)."

"Good-bye, Corrie, until we meet again, when we will be translated to meet the Lord in the sky."

10

Tell Me of Jesus

Oh, use me, Lord, use even me. Just as Thou wilt,
and when, and where.

On the platform the choir, in brownish red gowns,
stands behind me; a lady in a white gown is con-
ducting. I can study her while she conducts the choir.
Her appearance is unusual. She wears a lot of jewelry,
and gracefully moves her beautiful arms, which are deco-
rated with diamond bracelets. She wears brilliant rings on
her fingers; her nails are red. Her shoes are transparent.
But the most unusual thing about her is her smile. She
smiles in a coquettish manner when the tenors make a
mistake, encouragingly when a passage is difficult, and
coquettishly again when she has nothing else to do.

It is strange to see such a worldly woman taking part
in the sacred service. Looking at her, she appears to me to
be representative of the movie world, where coquettish
women play a big part. Suddenly she sings together with
the choir. She has a beautiful voice. Although she stands
with her back to the congregation, her solo can be heard
above the voices of the choir. For a time I am so absorbed
in her appearance that I do not hear what they are singing.
Now I listen to the words. She sings, "Tell me of Jesus."

My mind wanders. I am no longer in the church. Those words go round and round in my mind. Hollywood demands, "Tell me of Jesus." The sentenced-to-death, desperate, painted society says, "Tell me of Jesus."

When some moments later I stand before the congregation to bring them my message, in my heart there is a longing—a prayer. "Let me, this woman, and the movie world in Hollywood, tell of Jesus; of Him who came because the Father loved this poor, bad, desperate world."

Because of my background of imprisonment and world traveling, I sometimes arrive at places where doors do not open easily.

I stand before a hearth. In front of me sit fifty movie stars. The Hollywood Christian Group is having their gospel meeting. About twenty of their members are present; the rest are friends and acquaintances who do not yet know the Lord. We are in the house of a rich movie star. One of those present has a strong lamp, which she focuses on me and studies the effect.

I speak about the great love of God in Jesus Christ who can lift us out of the old vicious circle of sin and death. The Holy Spirit convinces us of sin, righteousness, and judgment. The greatest sin is not believing in Jesus.

After the meeting, little groups of people form. I see that the Christians are active and busy with open Bibles showing their colleagues the way of salvation.

I go with a young woman for a little walk on the terrace.

She has many questions to ask. Passing a window, I see two young men on their knees. One is a member of the Christian Group, the other a movie star who is making the decision that makes angels rejoice.

What a joy that God answers prayer!

11

Egotism

My thoughts are not your thoughts, neither are your ways My ways, saith the LORD.

Isaiah 55:8

At Havana, in Cuba, I am to speak at a youth rally in the Salvation Army hall. It is very hot, and the hall is small. The meeting begins at seven o'clock, but more and more groups continue to arrive from other parts of the town. Two men have huge drums, and I am sitting on the platform between them. An old Negro with white hair tries to show his love for the Lord by vigorously beating one of the drums. The sound is almost unbearable. The Captain has a very sharp voice, and the young Cubans sing loudly, with much clapping of hands. By nine o'clock I am feeling weary and my head is aching, but while I am speaking it is quiet in the hall, and I am thankful for this chance to give my message, which is followed by a missionary showing slides.

He is a little bit proud of his medical work, for which he has not studied specifically, but he, like all missionaries, must know enough to be able to act in cases of emergency. He has photographs of tables full of drugs. "These were given to me by Dr. Smith," he tells us. The young people in the hall are not at all interested in seeing these boxes, bottles, and vials, and the noise they are making grows to such a volume that the missionary has to shout to make himself heard at all. It is half past ten by the time he has finished.

Now the Captain gives an invitation to people to come to the front and be saved. A terribly selfish thought comes into my head. "I hope that nobody comes to the front. I long to go to bed."

Twenty young people come out. I see tears in the eyes of a young Cuban. The officer next to him speaks with great persuasion; his voice is full of love.

I am shocked by my selfishness. I had hoped that nobody would be saved because my own sleep was more important than the salvation of sinners. What a terrible egotist I am! But what a joy that I know what to do with my sin. I confess it to my heavenly Father in Jesus' name, and he forgives and cleanses me. Then with joy I can pray for the twenty young people who have made the important decision. It is half past eleven when the meeting comes to a close.

The next morning I am standing in a beautifully designed church, which the most prominent people of Havana attend. In the parish magazine, given to everyone who enters, I read an introductory article on Corrie ten Boom. It says: "Most popular world evangelist . . . tireless and completely selfless in her absolute dedication to the cause of the gospel!" Before I give my message, I cannot help reading the introduction aloud, and continue, "Sometimes I get a headache from the heat of the halo that people put around my head. Would you like to know what Corrie ten Boom is really like?" And then I tell them what happened the evening before, of how my own sleep was more important in my eyes than the salvation of young people. "That," I say, "is Corrie ten Boom. What egotism! What selfishness! But the joy is that Corrie ten Boom knows what to do with her sins. When we confess our sins to the heavenly Father, we experience that our Advocate lives—Jesus Christ. He takes our sins on Himself."

Suddenly there is contact with the congregation. We are no longer a beautiful church with prominent members and a popular world evangelist, but we are all sinners who know that Jesus died to lift us out of the vicious circle of sin and death.

12

San Bartolo de la Barranca

Life is too short to be little.

W hat do you use that knife for?"
To defend myself against robbers and wild animals; but today I have to cut the cacti that can be dangerous to the clothing and the skin of Miss Corrie ten Boom."

I follow the Mexican with his big hat and his long knife. I have never seen such a long knife before. It is very sharp, and pieces of cacti fall around him until we reach the edge of the canyon. Far down below, people are working to make a way to a town in the valley. This was once the center of crime, of murder, and theft. It was so difficult to reach that only a few people knew of its existence. Then about eight years ago, God gave some Christians the idea to go and live there, where "Satan's seat" was (Revelation 2:13). They could reach the town only by a very tiring journey on horseback through woods and dangerous cliffs.

The first thing they did was to rent the public house for a meeting. When customers came, they told them, "Wait until we have finished with you!" The persecution they had to suffer was terrible, but they stood their ground. Within a short time God performed miracles, and now it is a Christian town. The mayor is the minister, the judge is his assistant, and all the policemen are deacons.

Although it is rather far away, I can see a huge flat church. It is a strange building but with room for many. The people saw the dangers of isolation and tried to make contact with other Christians whom they invited to come and see them. The bravest of these found a chance to visit the town, but the trip on horseback was dangerous and unbelievably difficult. So the Christians promised their visitors that if they would try to come back the following year they would make a way through the jungle.

This plan was made known, and the government of the state asked if it was true that Christians were making a highway through the jungle, though "highway" is too good a name for the rough road they hacked through the wilderness. The Christians were glad to give information to the government and said that they were willing to work without payment, but that they had no money to cover the costs. The government official was so impressed that he promised material and instructors to help with the work.

The main work is under the supervision of the instructors; dynamite and tools have been given by the state, and the Christians from 130 different congregations cooperate in doing the work. Each congregation contributes one week's labor. Women come together with the men to cook for them and take care of them. A text is painted on a rock in huge letters, "WE WORK FOR GOD AND NOT FOR MEN."

In this Roman Catholic country Protestants are sometimes in a difficult position. Already the work of these faithful Christians has caused the government to see with amazement how useful they can be to society. A congress of mayors was invited to see the work, and on that day the first bridge was opened; on it is carved, "WHAT YOU DO, DO WITH YOUR WHOLE HEART."

An old man with a long beard takes me to the workers. He climbs with difficulty down the steep mountain. When the men in the valley see us they shout, "Hallelujah!" and we answer with the same salute. The sound echoes between the mountains. "Hallelujah! Hallelujah! Hallelujah!"

In the camp where the women live a meal has been made for us. One woman rolls a stone over the corn while another bakes the flat tortillas. The whole camp is rather dirty, but the atmosphere is happy, and what faithfulness!

"Do all the members of the church come to take their part in the work?" I ask.

"Yes! But if one did fail, another immediately would take his place. They say, 'We work because we love God and our neighbors, and we will serve society.'"

Within two years there will be a highway connecting San Bartolo de la Barranca with the big world. Poverty will decrease when there is the possibility of trade, but people expect far more than that: that this town will be a pleasing example to all who come into contact with it.

When I leave, I say a few words of farewell— 1 John 5:4–5: "This is the victory that overcometh the world, even our faith. Who is he that overcometh the world, but he that believeth that Jesus is the Son of God?" Here is a little foretaste of the millennium, when the children of God will reign on this earth with Jesus Christ, and the whole world shall be "full of the knowledge of the Lord, as the waters cover the sea."

13

Wiener Roast

He that winneth souls is wise.

Proverbs 11:30

In America when people go for a picnic they travel by car. How unlike the Europeans, who walk and carry their knapsacks on their backs. Sometimes I fear that Americans are unable to walk! Their cars take them everywhere.

I go to a wiener roast with the youth groups of a church. We cook the wieners over the fire on spiked sticks cut from the trees. It is a jolly group of people. After the picnic we sit around the fire and the conversation is about soul-winning. A girl student says, "I am no evangelist and have no guidance to go to a Bible school, but I speak with a lot of young people whom I like to help. Do you know of a good book about soul-winning?"

"Yes, several. One is *The Consuming Fire* by Oswald J. Smith. He writes a chapter called 'Evangelism in the Enquiry Room,' which is a short but powerful guide for soul-winning in personal conversation.

"First, he says, never argue. Many people will try to argue to avoid the important thing. They ask the most impossible questions. Don't try to answer them. Promise to do that later, but first show them that they need salvation.

"Also, trust the Holy Spirit. Only He can convince of sin and change people—you can't.

"Pray a great deal. Pray before, during, and after your conversation. It is possible that you need exercise, but you can have the horizontal and the vertical connection at the same time.

"Make your diagnosis and seek the remedy. Let the Bible speak.

"Sometimes you can find four groups—the unsaved, the backsliders, the uncertain, and the defeated.

"First, the unsaved, who do not know the Lord Jesus Christ can be their personal Savior, who do not call themselves Christians. They must be invited to repent. Read with them John 1:12: 'But as many as received Him, to them gave He power to become the sons of God, even to them that believe on His name.'

"Then the backsliders. They have slid away from the Lord. They have lost their first love and are cold in their work for the gospel, neglect their Bible reading and prayer, and never witness. Some live totally in the world. They must be brought back again to fellowship with God. The reason for their backsliding is always sin. Read with them 1 John 1:7–9. Show them that they must confess the sins that have made them backslide. In case they do not feel any joy after their confession of sins, tell them to thank God for forgiveness. Often the joy comes only after they have given thanks with their hands on the promises of the Bible.

"The third group is the uncertain—those who do not know if they are saved or lost. They have no assurance of salvation, feeling one day that they are children of God, and the next that they are lost. They are in a state of permanent uncertainty. They must be invited to come back because they have no value for God until they know that they have passed from darkness into light. Tell them that they must not trust their feelings, but God's Word.

> Feelings come, and feelings go,
> And feelings are deceiving.
> My warrant is the Word of God
> None else is worth believing.

"Let them read 1 John 5:13: 'These things have I written unto you that believe on the name of the Son of God: that ye may know that ye have eternal life, and that ye may believe on the name of the Son of God.' Not feelings, or wonderful emotional experiences, or unusual revelations, but 'It is written.'

"What is written cannot be changed. Feelings and emotions can change. Teach them to act on the Word. Christians are not always on the mountaintop. If there were no valleys, there could be no mountains. If our feelings were the foundation, then we could be a child of God only if we were on the mountain. John says, 'These things have I written.' What has he written? 'That ye know that ye have eternal life.' Not that you may have everlasting life some day, but that you have it here and now. It is very important to show the uncertain these things in the Word of God. God can't use uncertain people. Those who have no assurance of salvation can't help others. They must know that they have passed from darkness into light, and that knowledge comes by faith in what the Bible says.

"Then we have the defeated. Show them

1 Corinthians 15:57: 'Thanks be to God, which giveth us the victory through our Lord Jesus Christ.' Not by trying hard, by our endeavors or our energy, but by Him, our Lord. Victory is a gift just like salvation—we can't earn it. God gives it to us by His Son. Even Paul cried, 'O wretched man that I am! who shall deliver me from the body of this death?' (Romans 7:24), but immediately added, 'I thank God through Jesus Christ our Lord.'

"We have accepted Jesus as our Savior; now we must accept Him as our Victor. When we do this He lives His victorious life in us—He the Vine, we the branches. The branch without the Vine has no value, but the Vine has everlasting value. When connected with the Vine, the branch gets the same nature, and life, and zeal to bear fruit like the Vine itself. 'Without Me ye can do nothing,' Jesus says. But I can do everything through Christ, who gives me strength. Hallelujah!"

During our talk, the fire has died down. We see clearly the beautiful starry sky. Before we leave, we sing together:

Is your life a channel of blessing?
Is the love of God flowing through you?
Are you telling the lost of the Savior?
Are you ready His service to do?

Make me a channel of blessing today,
Make me a channel of blessing, I pray;
My life possessing, my service blessing,
Make me a channel of blessing today.

14

Ingredients for Prayer

All promises of God are in Jesus, yea and amen.

In the cell of a prison a woman lies on her cot with a bored expression on her face. She has a cheap novel in her hand, but it does not interest her much. Her needlework lies neglected on her chair. It is warm, and it is Sunday. Does she miss her daily work, which, although monotonous, helps her to get through the day? She is Dutch but has not attended my meeting.

I am visiting the cells after the sermon—an unusual privilege. Although I am allowed to speak at meetings in prisons, the follow-up work is usually left to the regular prison evangelists. I sit near the Dutch woman, and for a short time can share her life in the small cell—colorless, monotonous, without any view. I know so well what it is like from my own experience. I feel such great love and compassion for this woman and pray that the Lord will give me entrance to her heart.

The ice is broken sooner than I expect, and we have a heart-to-heart talk. To begin with, the conversation is about baking cakes—a typical reaction engendered by the hunger that results from a monotonous diet. Carefully I try to turn our talk to deeper things. I discover that she has quite a good knowledge of the Bible, and it is easy to speak to her about the eternal truths. She knows that Jesus died for her on the cross, but she is a backslider.

"Do you sometimes make use of the time that you are alone to pray?" I ask.

"I don't know how to pray. Tell me something of your own prayer life."

"For cakes you need ingredients, and you need them for prayer too. For instance, the ingredients of a prayer could be:

1. The promises of God.
2. Our problems and needs.
3. Faith to bring these two together.

"If you don't understand me, I'll give you an example.

"Yesterday I was in darkness—really depressed. I didn't know what to do. When this happens I quietly spend a few minutes trying to find the reason. I can imagine a rich lady once a week gathering her bills together and writing out her checks. My Bible is my checkbook; my cares and problems are the bills. The devil tells me that the Bible is frozen capital, but he is a liar. All promises of God are in Jesus, yea and amen. I asked God to show me the reason for the darkness. God will give His children a clear answer when they are willing to listen in obedience. It is a question of making use of the quiet time. Then I wrote down the thoughts that came into my head. Finding the reason for the darkness is in itself a work of liberation. After making my list I took my Bible to 'pay my bills.'

"The first thing I had written was that I was afraid for my health. Next week I must go to Japan, and I wondered if my body would stand the different climate—I am no longer young. I read Romans 8:11: 'Nevertheless once the Spirit of Him who raised Jesus from the dead lives within you He will, by that same Spirit, bring to your whole being new strength and vitality' (PHILLIPS). I said, 'Thank You, Lord. That is for me.' That thank-you meant that I had endorsed a check.

"The next thing on my list was that I was feeling down-hearted. The church where I am speaking this week had organized a prayer meeting. I went to that meeting, but nobody else arrived. I had to pray alone. Then I read Romans 8:27: '[The Spirit] prays for those who love God,' and verse 34, 'Christ prays for us' (PHILLIPS). I understood then that there *had* been a prayer meeting, for if you are praying, the Lord is praying, and the Holy Spirit is praying, and that makes a prayer cell. I said, 'Thank You, Lord,' and another bill was paid.

"Third, there followed my feeling of guilt. I had been tempted to gossip. No, it was not slandering. Everything said was true, but it was negative. Paul writes in Romans 14, 'Why criticize your brother's actions? After all, who are you to criticize the servant of somebody else, especially when that somebody else is God? It is to his own Master that he gives, or fails to give, satisfactory service. And don't doubt that satisfaction, for God is well able to transform men into servants who are satisfactory' (PHILLIPS).

"There were other sins I had committed for the umpteenth time: worry, selfishness, etc. I read Romans 8:1: 'No condemnation now hangs over the head of those who are "in" Jesus Christ. For the new spiritual principle of life "in" Christ lifts me out of the old vicious circle of sin and death' (PHILLIPS). I said, 'Thank You, Lord. The devil is very strong, but You are victor.'

"The last thing I had written down was that deep in my heart I was afraid to go to Japan. I do not know the language, nor what awaits me there. I wondered if people would help me, and if I should be able to find my way about. What a shame to have such doubts. The Lord has carried me through a most terrible time in prison. Won't He take care of me in Japan? I read the words of victory at the end of Romans 8: 'Who shall separate us from the love of Christ? In all these things we are more than conquerors.' My last bill was paid, the checks written. The darkness was all gone. I saw again that God's promises are greater realities than our problems. How exceedingly rich we are when we do not limit the promises of the Bible by our unbelief."

"When you talk like this, I really start to long to live the Christian life again. I am going to do my best."

I look smilingly at her. "Do you see this stick? Do you think it is possible for it to stand upright on its own? Of course not, for it is not the nature of the stick to stand by itself. It can do so only when my hand keeps it steady. It is not the nature of human beings to be able to stand on their own. They can do it only when they surrender to the hand that will keep them from falling. Look, here in Jude, verse 24: 'Now to Him who is able to keep you from falling and to present you before His glory without fault and with unspeakable joy' (PHILLIPS)."

For a moment we are quiet together, and I know that the Holy Spirit works in her heart. Then she surrenders to the hand that was wounded to save her.

I write in her Bible:

It is not try, but trust.
It is not do, but done.
Our God has planned for us
Great victory through His Son.

15

Obedience

Our eyes must be turned toward God as the eyes of
the musician are turned toward the conductor.

It is a wonderful life that is guided by a God who never
makes mistakes. The only condition laid upon us is
obedience.

"When are you going to bring this message to the
Japanese?" a friend asks me after he hears one of my lec-
tures. Until then I have worked only in America and
Europe, Japan being far from my thoughts.

In my quiet time the instruction comes distinctly: "Go
to Japan." I almost answer, "Yes, but . . ." Obedience says,
"Yes, Lord," and I have learned to obey. I want to say,
"Yes, but I know nobody there; I can't speak the language
and it is so expensive." Again and again I begin counting
and forget that my heavenly treasurer reckons differently
from me. The money comes, enough for a flight to Tokyo,
where I arrive safely.

It is raining, and from the air Tokyo looks dark and
dreary. I am not at all sure of myself. In the customs
office a man asks me where he is to take my suitcase. I
tell him I do not know.

"Is someone going to meet you?"

"No; nobody."

He feels sorry for me and offers to find me a hotel.

"Yes, if you please—and if possible one where English, German, or Dutch is spoken."

In his own car he takes me to a hotel. It is small, dirty, and dark, but the manager understands some English. But now there is a conflict in my soul. Was that really God's guidance? What if it was a mistake? I hardly dare to go out of doors for fear I might lose my way back to the hotel. Who would understand me? It becomes a real temptation from Satan. How terribly God's children are tempted in these times. It is as though Satan knows his time is running out. Then I read 1 Peter 1 in Phillips's *Letters to Young Churches* about the glorious inheritance reserved in heaven for me, and in the meantime we are guarded by God's power until we enter fully into that heritage—the only life insurance we can collect after our death.

"This means tremendous joy to you, I know, even though at present you are temporarily harassed by all kinds of trials and temptations. This is *no accident*—it happens to prove your faith, which is infinitely more valuable than gold, and gold as you know, even though it is ultimately perishable, must be purified by fire. This proving of your faith is *planned* to bring you praise and honor and glory in the day when Jesus Christ reveals Himself" (1 Peter 1:6–7 PHILLIPS).

No accident—planned! Not by accident, God's plan? But why? To bring praise and glory on the great day of Christ's return. How glorious to catch a glimpse of that great plan and to see your own troubles as a tiny part of that plan. God makes no mistakes!

How it happens I cannot explain, but trust takes the

place of doubt, and I can say, "Lord, I know I am safe in Your everlasting arms. You are guiding me and will surely make the next step plain."

Then comes to mind: "David Morken." Is that God's answer? Years ago I met David at a Youth for Christ meeting, and he told me then that he might be sent to Japan. Fortunately the telephone directory is printed in English, and there is his name, "David Morken, Director of Youth for Christ, Tokyo."

How wonderful, for now the next step is clear. I pick up the telephone and hear a voice saying, "Mashie, mashie, mushie, mushie." In confusion I replace the receiver. I cannot even telephone in this strange land of strange people speaking a strange language. Finally, the manager gets the number for me, and I speak to David Morken.

"Hello. This is Corrie ten Boom speaking."

"What! Where are you?"

"Here in Tokyo."

"With whom?"

"Alone."

"But Corrie, how could you? You can't speak Japanese. If this isn't just like you, to come alone to a country where you can't understand the language!"

"It isn't my doing. I'm not enjoying this at all. It is God's doing, sending me here."

"Okay. Always obey what God tells you to do. I'll help you. Go to the Central Railway Station, and I'll meet you with my car."

He did not offer to come to the hotel because it is hard to locate places in Tokyo. The first house built in a street is No. 1, the second, No. 2, even though it may be half a mile farther down the street. Hence numbers mean nothing.

"How do I find the station?"

"Take a taxi."

"What must I say to the taxi driver?"

"Ekki." And true enough, I call a taxi and just say, "Ekki," and eventually arrive at the station, where David Morken awaits me. That day I am his guest, after which he secures a room for me in an Inter-Varsity Christian Fellowship house.

The first week I speak three times, the second week eighteen times, and the third week twenty-six times. A season of unusual blessing awaits me. How happy I am that I said "Yes, Lord" instead of "Yes, but . . ."

One of the greatest blessings in Japan is that God uses me to help His special messengers, the missionaries. I am able to give them inspiration and show them from my own experiences that Jesus' victory is a greater reality than our problems.

Many missionaries have to spend their first years in Japan learning the language. This period can be very trying, for they cannot play their real part. They go to a heathen land with hearts burning to save souls for eternity, and then they must sit on school benches and learn the difficult language. Let us be very faithful in our intercession for them, for it is a time when many are assailed by doubts as to whether, after all, it really was God's will for them to undertake the work.

To a group of political prisoners I speak about the forgiveness of sins. The next day a letter written in perfect Dutch comes with the request, "Will you write to your Queen for me? She is the only one who can grant me amnesty." The writer is one of 260 Japanese prisoners sentenced by the Dutch government for war crimes in Indonesia, once the Dutch East Indies. They are now in a Japanese prison.

I hardly know what to do. Lacking an answer, I follow Hezekiah's example, when during the siege of Jerusalem he received that threatening letter from Rabshakeh, and "spread it before the Lord."

"What must I do, Lord?" I ask.

The answer comes clearly. "Ask amnesty not only for this man, but for all 260."

I go to the consul to seek his help in composing my letter, for it is not every day I write to a queen. "These men are guilty," I write, "but in you they see the Christian monarch of a Christian country. Perhaps they can better understand the mercy of our Lord Jesus if you can see your way clear to grant them their freedom, and so it will be to God's glory and honor."

The Queen sends me the answer that she will do her utmost to see that my request is granted, but at least two years expire before the men are freed.

However, that week I am called before the committee responsible for all prisoners in Japan. A permit is given me to speak in all prisons; in fact, an itinerary is mapped out for me. I can count on their full cooperation in appreciation for what I did for their political prisoners. What a blessing! When a missionary or pastor speaks, each inmate is asked whether he is interested in the Christian religion. Often only a handful shows up at meetings. But since my work is considered more or less official, attendance is compulsory for all prisoners, and at times also for the attendants. What an opportunity!

The prisons are often far apart. Life is now very different from what I experienced in Tokyo. In large cities the customs and manners of Europeans are well known, and the Japanese are the most polite people in the world. So, when a guest in a Japanese home, I am often offered a chair, though it is their custom to sit on the floor, and often I find a spoon beside my plate that I may eat in comfortable European fashion instead of handling chopsticks. But now the carefully laid plan takes me far away from the large cities. A police wagon meets me at the station and carries me to the prison. Frequently I ride in jeeps over rough roads. The bouncing is good exercise, I tell myself, but somehow I do not appreciate it.

Usually a dinner has been prepared in my honor. The warden and officials sit with me on the floor, and we eat with chopsticks. The Japanese are well read, and the conversation is stimulating. They speak of "Het Spinhuis," the reformatory in Amsterdam, where back in the sixteenth century prisoners were not only held but also educated at the same time. They appreciate the Dutch, who even in those early days saw the possibilities, now universally accepted, in educating prisoners. I had hardly expected conversation of this kind in these remote corners of Japan's northernmost island.

"Today you will address one hundred and forty gangsters," the warden warns me. There they sit closely packed on the floor, long rows of Japanese sitting on their heels. My first reaction is, "What darkness!" Cruel faces stare at me.

The lost ones! The world has only one answer, to keep them behind barbed wire. Then great joy rises in my heart. I have a message for them, the answer to their problems. An ocean of sin and darkness was covered with a greater ocean of love and light when Jesus died on the cross. It was for them He died and bore the sins of the whole world.

I tell them of this ocean of love. "Your souls are precious in the sight of God. Accept Jesus as your Lord and Savior and He will give you power to become children of God. The tender father-heart of God yearns for your love."

I can almost see the faces change. I see God's love at work, and His love overflows in my heart as never before. What great riches! The prisoners applaud. It is the only expression allowed them, and their applause is long and loud.

Since there is no hotel, the interpreter and I are guests at the governer's home. At dinner that evening he says, "While you were speaking, the thought came to me that I, too, would like to be saved."

"That is possible. Jesus died for the sins of the whole world, yours included. Believe on the Lord Jesus Christ and you shall be saved."

"I am thinking of choosing a savior for myself, but haven't made up my mind whether it shall be Christ or Buddha. It really does not matter which, does it, as long as we are sincere?"

"You think it does not matter?" I pray for wisdom and remember an illustration.

"Two men were building a house. Suddenly the scaffolding broke. One man grabbed a rope that was firmly fastened and saved his life. The other grabbed a rope also, but it was loose, and he fell with the rope to the ground and was killed. If you choose Jesus as Savior you will be saved for time and eternity. But if you choose Buddha I fear you will be eternally lost. Do you believe that Buddha is alive?"

His answer is typical. "You will have to ask the Commissioner of Education. He knows all about Buddha—I know nothing about him."

"Do you believe that Jesus lives?"

"Yes, I'm sure of it. I saw it in the prisoners' eyes when you spoke about Him."

"Why, then, is it so difficult to choose? You know Jesus lives and don't know whether Buddha is alive or not."

"No, that choice isn't so difficult," he says, and after we pray he makes the decision that causes the angels in heaven to rejoice.

Later, he asks, "Is there anything else I can do for you?'

"Yes. Perhaps there are prisoners who would like to meet me. I am so eager to help them further. After all, one talk is so little." And indeed there are fourteen who wish to speak to me, and a whole hour is granted me, even though it is against the rules that prisoners leave their cells after five o'clock. I feel I must make the most of every minute.

"Friends, it would take me months to teach you all I feel you should know, but we have just one hour. Tell me, which of you care to make the decision for the Lord of whom John says: 'As many as received Him, to them gave He power to become the sons of God' (1 John 1:12)?"

"We all have; that's why we are here," one replies.

"Very well, there is work to be done. You must be ambassadors for Christ. There are many souls to be rescued for eternity in this prison. I shall send you a Bible and a course of Bible study. To begin with, here are eight selections that you can use to bring others to Christ:

John 1:12	Romans 3:23
John 3:16	1 Timothy 1:15
John 6:37	1 John 1:7, 9
John 14:6	Revelation 3:20

"When you have finished the first Bible study course I shall send you another in soul-winning. In the meantime you must be the intercessors for the rest of the prisoners. For instance, you assemble together at mealtimes. Perhaps you could arrange to sit together as Christians and form prayer cells. Pray together for five minutes, or even one minute if that is all you can manage. Jesus has said, 'Where two or three are gathered together in My name, there am I in the midst of them.'

"I know how you feel when you are alone in your prison cells after five o'clock. I myself spent four months in solitary confinement. That is the time to pray for others. Pray for your fellow-prisoners, especially those to whom you have brought the gospel. Pray for the attendants and for your dear ones at home, if you still have them. There is much to be done for the Master, but remember He can use only those who are pure in heart. That, too, is possible for you. Just confess your sins. Anyone who confesses his sins will find God faithful to forgive them, and the blood of Jesus cleanses from *all* sin. When you confess, He will give you the new heart in which He wishes to dwell. But you must never, never compromise."

We have a moment of silence and then we give thanks together.

"Now," I ask, "who has given himself unconditionally to the Lord?" Fourteen hands are raised in firm and full surrender.

Fourteen gangsters, murderers! Fourteen lifers!

Fourteen despised, lost men? No, fourteen ambassadors for Christ.

Shall they one day hear the words, "Well done, thou good and faithful servant: thou hast been faithful over a few things, I will make thee ruler over many things"?

Shall I see them one day, with those they have brought to the Lord?

A year later I receive a letter with some money enclosed. It is from one of the prisoners. He writes, "I have been unexpectedly set free. I have found work, and the first money I have earned in my freedom I am sending to you. Please send me a Bible. The balance of the money is for your work.

"When you spoke to us in prison I accepted Jesus as my Savior. I served Him behind the bars, and now I plan to serve Him as a free man."

I write to a missionary commending this former prisoner to the fellowship of a live congregation and suggesting he be put to work there for his Master. What a privilege to see some of the blessed fruit the Vine has given through the branches.

16

The Power of Jesus' Name

The true child of God . . . is in the charge of God's own Son and the evil one must keep his distance.

1 John 5:18 PHILLIPS

How difficult it is to become used to speaking through interpreters. It is like trying to reach for people round a corner. The listener's eyes being on the interpreter, the speaker is more or less out of touch with his audience. It has one virtue, however; there is time for prayer while speaking.

Today I have an especially fine interpreter. He loves the Lord with all his heart, and it is pure delight to work together—such a contrast to indifferent interpreters. We are guests in the same home, and since we must speak again in the evening, there is time to chat together. Suddenly I ask, "Why is there so much darkness in you?"

"What do you mean?"

"There is no joy of the Lord in your eyes. In the parable of the vine and the branches, the Lord says, 'That My joy might remain in you, and that your joy might be full.' Where is that joy?"

"I don't know."

"I think perhaps I know. May I speak? When you

were converted from Shintoism to the Lord, you turned your back on demons, but the demons have not turned their backs on you."

In surprise he answers, "That is true. But please don't tell the missionaries. They may think I've gone back to Shintoism."

"Demons are no ism. They are realities even as angels, and as you and I are. What you lack is a knowledge of the riches that are yours. You need not remain in darkness one moment longer. In the name of the Lord Jesus and by the blood of the Lamb we have the victory. In His name you can drive out the demons and withstand Satan."

Together we read and obey the glorious promise and command in Mark 16:15–18, and then the Lord performs the miracle of the complete liberation of His child.

A few weeks later we meet again. "Not only am I free," he says, "but my wife and children also." All hail the power of Jesus' name! The wonderful name of Jesus is all power-ful in heaven and on earth. That name above every name.

Many missionaries have *given* their all—money, family, and homeland—but they do not *take* all the riches offered them in God's Word. Theologically their training has often been basic, but would not a study of God's Word teaching them to cast out demons and heal the sick make them more fruitful?

How many dark powers there are in the world! Yet we have nothing to fear. The fear of demons is from the demons themselves. We overcome by the blood of the Lamb, and His blood protects us. And what joy it is that we have the authority of the name of Jesus.

Those who are with us are far more than those who are against us. At our side is our mighty High Priest and His legions of angels.

17

⊷

That Intercession Be Made

I measure my influence by the number who need my prayers and the number who pray for me.

Tokyo is noisy. Loudspeakers screaming shrill music in the streets sound above the hubbub below. Opposite the house where I live is a school of music. It is July and steaming hot. Windows are wide open everywhere, and the mingled sounds of trumpets, harmonicas, and violins fling their clamor into my hot room. It is almost unbearable. Evenings are hours of affliction, for all things seem to work together for evil. Previously I lived with four missionaries, one a woman who, with the help of a Japanese girl, took charge of the cooking. We had delightful meals due more to the fine fellowship around the tiny table in that small room with its mat-covered floor than to the quality of the food. Happily for me I could throw off the burden of past experiences as together we read the Bible, related difficulties, and praised the Lord for blessings shared with His children.

But now I am alone. The others have left for a cooler climate in the hills while I must complete several series of lectures in the university, a Bible seminary, and a student's club. I try cooking in the queer kitchen, but have not much success. I am not very skilled in the science of cooking, and evidently the Japanese idea of hygiene differs from mine, for somehow everything I cook tastes of fish. A cockroach scuttles from the wardrobe after chewing holes in my very best dress. I begin to lose heart.

The nights seem unendurably hot. The unscreened windows invite swarms of mosquitoes. Self-pity rises in my heart and whispers, "Why must I work here when the heat is so overpowering? I'm no longer young, and adjustment does not come easily. Why must I be alone? Why? Why? It's just too bad, Corrie!"

Self-pity creates darkness and can even cause sickness. It is a very respectable sin, logical and convincing, and places self on the throne.

One evening all the neighbors turn up their radios to drown the cacophony from the school of music. It is too much. No human being can bear this!

Suddenly I look into the mirror and burst out laughing. What a long face! How foolish to feel so sorry for myself. I try singing above the clamor, and sure enough, it works. The heat of the night can be endured, after all, for a prayer rises in my heart, "Lord Jesus, You suffered so much to save me from sin and make me a child of Yours. Why shouldn't I endure a bit of discomfort in carrying Your message to others? It is well, Lord. You had no place to lay Your head. I have a bed, and a room, even though they are both filled with mosquitoes."

A fortnight later a letter from Toronto reaches me. A friend writes, "Today an acquaintance phoned and asked me if I knew you. I told her we were friends. She has never met you but has just finished reading your book *Amazing Love* and since then has been in prayer for you all day long. I asked her to visit me, and together we prayed for you."

Is it not wonderful! We read in Isaiah 59:16, "And God wondered that there was no intercessor." How important is intercession. In Tokyo a child of God loses heart and falls into the sin of self-pity. Of course God can save her, but first He sends a command to Toronto, "Pray for her." And not until two of His children obey does He rescue Corrie ten Boom in Tokyo.

So are God's ways.

18

The Lily of the Valley Club

What heroes there are in God's kingdom!

In a street in Japan I meet some boys and girls with baskets full of tracts and Gospels of John. They seek to leave in every home a Gospel and a tract. They work to a well-organized plan, and after they have spent every Saturday afternoon for ten months, each house in Nagaoka will have a Gospel of John.

They are just children, but the Lord uses them. They call themselves "The Lily of the Valley Club." The leader is an eighteen-year-old boy, Daniel. He was once an opium smoker. The moment that he received the Lord Jesus he was free and now works full-time for the Lord and the church.

In one of the houses is a woman who years ago was a Christian, but she has turned away from the Lord. She finds the Gospel of John and starts to read. The Holy Spirit uses this reading, and later she calls her husband and children and tells them what she has read. She visits the minister, and now the whole family goes to church.

In heaven The Lily of the Valley Club will hear from several sides, "It was you who invited me here!"

There is a Bible woman who visits every week sixteen

different villages to bring them the gospel. She is a sick woman with tuberculosis in both lungs.

"I can't go to bed and be ill as long as there are so many people who don't know the Lord," she says to me.

What heroes there are in God's kingdom!

A little boy, Steven, cannot yet go to school because he is too young; only five years old. He is a clever little man, and therefore his mother, an American missionary, teaches him the Japanese language to keep him busy. Steven tells me, "I learn Japanese because I'll be a missionary."

"What about Russia, Steven? Won't you be a missionary there?"

"Sure I will!" says the little boy.

"But then you must learn Russian also. Are you willing?"

"Mummy, don't you think it is better that I wait until I am six?'

19

⊶∾⊷

The Winning Blow

If you will work for God, form a committee.
If you will work with God, form a prayer group.

During my trip from Formosa to Australia, I am able to stay for five days in Hong Kong. This beautiful island has riches and poverty side by side. It has the most beautiful window displays in the world, but also many slums full of refugees. It is a piece of free China with huge problems.

My time there is full of activity. I am in contact with many consecrated Christians. The meetings are extremely well organized, every minute of the day being put to good use.

One evening the Holy Spirit is obviously working in a group of young Christians who some time ago accepted Jesus Christ as their Savior. On this particular evening they come to a full surrender, and accept Him as their Victor. "Thanks be to God, which giveth us the victory through our Lord Jesus Christ" (1 Corinthians 15:57).

One asks, "What is expected of us now?"

"The Lord will show you. Wait patiently for His guidance. But there is one thing I can advise you to do now, and that is to organize prayer cells. Prayer is not a prefix or a suffix; it is central. Over the whole world I see that God gives His children prayer cells. It is not only the communists who form cells, but wherever two or three come together in Jesus' name, there is a cell for Him. In eternity we shall see how important prayer meetings have been."

A group of students in Chicago prayed every week for a number of unsaved fellow students. Eventually everyone on the list was saved. One of them was Dr. Torrey Johnson, the founder of Youth for Christ. Wherever I have traveled over the world I have seen how this work has been blessed. Thousands and tens of thousands have found their Savior through it. What was the first cause? Torrey Johnson? No, the prayers of those young men in Chicago. Intercession is so tremendously important that in Isaiah 59:16 is written, "God wondered that there was no intercessor."

"If you will work for God, form a committee. If you will work with God, form a prayer group."

That evening, we make plans for a weekly prayer meeting, and later I hear that more have commenced. The greatest thing we can do for one another is to pray. Prayer is striking the winning blow at the concealed enemy—our service is gathering up the results.

20

Boomerang

The first step on the way to victory is to recognize the enemy.

At a conference of Bible school students it is necessary to have somebody to interpret for me, and this is done by a girl who finds it difficult to understand my English. When I use an illustration involving radar in ships she becomes quite mixed up, as she has never heard of radar before. I try to help her, and say, "It doesn't matter; we will try something else. A captain of a ship stood on the bridge . . ." but she has never heard of the bridge of a ship, and does not say a word. I tell her, "Read Phillips's translation of James 1:5. 'If . . . any of you does not know how to meet any particular problem he has only to ask God—who gives generously to all men without making them feel foolish or guilty—and he may be quite sure that the necessary wisdom will be given him.' You lack the wisdom to interpret for Corrie ten Boom. This is the address where you can get it."

But it is too late. She bursts into tears. A Japanese who loses face is lost; you cannot do anything with him. I ask the leader of the conference if there is another interpreter, but he tells me there is not. So here I am with a message for the young people before me. Some of them have problems, and the answers can be found in the Bible that I have in my hand.

For what reason am I unable to bring God's message to them? Here is the devil at work. The first step on the way to victory is to recognize the enemy. The devil is a conquered enemy, and we have the privilege and the authority to fight him in the name of the Lord Jesus. I turn to the girl and say, "Dark power that hinders this girl from interpreting God's message—I command you in the name of the Lord Jesus to leave her alone. She is meant to be a temple of the Holy Spirit, not your temple."

As I speak, the girl is set free. She is able to interpret fluently, and we have a meeting that is greatly blessed. So what the devil has meant to be an illustration of his victory becomes a boomerang and shows the power of Jesus Christ and His name.

21

Lailani

Do not be a victim of activity. When Satan cannot make you bad, he makes you busy.

Honolulu is a beautiful island. What riches of sun and color! Nature gives an overflow of flowers the whole year round. The blue water, the mountains—it really makes a symphony in clear colors. Young people decorate themselves with flower chains sometimes made of beautiful orchids, and these they also wear in their hair. Their clothing is multicolored. The life of the tourist is frivolous, but I come into contact more with the Christians, who educate their children carefully and keep them away from the tourist world. There are several Bible study and prayer groups.

One evening the conversation is about prayer. Lailani says, "I think it is very difficult to pray."

"No wonder. Even the disciples did not find it easy. They asked the Lord to teach them how to pray. It is a strategic point. The devil smiles when we are up to our ears in work, but he trembles when we pray. Sometimes I think that there must be a map of the world both in heaven and in hell. The most important points on the map are not the Kremlin in Moscow, or the Pentagon building in Washington, but the places where two or three or more are gathered in Jesus' name in prayer meetings."

When the Americans entered Germany after the war, a law was made forbidding fraternization. In one minister's family were two teenage children. At school they had heard terrible things about the Americans. One day the girls saw an American officer coming toward their house and cried, "Look, father. He is coming to our house."

"Don't be afraid. Americans are not barbarians."

The officer entered the house, and when he came into their room, said, "We are forbidden to speak and eat together, but nobody has forbidden us to pray together."

He knelt down, and the minister and his family followed. Into the hearts of the children at that moment came a great love for the Americans. Prayer is like Jacob's ladder. Angels go up and down, but it is God who places the ladder.

"But I find I have no time to pray," says Lailani.

"You remind me of a German minister with far too big a congregation who said he was really too busy to pray. He had plenty of theology but no 'kneeology.' That is just as fruitless as a beautiful lamp without electricity.

"My full schedule and constant traveling from one place to another can sometimes bring me into the same danger. In the morning I must awaken early to travel; in the evening I roll into bed dead tired. On such occasions I have really tried to find time to pray until I have seen that prayerlessness is a sin. I know what to do with sins. I do not try to overcome them, but face them, and 1 John 1:7–9 gives the answer. A sin confessed to the Lord is a sin forgiven; a sin forgiven is a sin cleansed. In the same moment that I confessed my prayerlessness I found time to pray.

"Trying to catch up on our prayers while sitting in the bus or train or airplane after the day's work has begun is a poor substitute. We must begin the day by tuning our instruments with the help of the great Conductor. Prayer is the key for the day; the lock for the night. When Satan cannot keep us from doing work for the Lord he comes behind us and pushes us into doing too much work, and much we do is not right. In that case we must pray with the man who was too busy, and who said:

Slow me down, Lord, I'm going too fast,
I can't see my brother when he's going
    past;
I miss a lot of good things day by day,
I can't see a blessing when it comes my
    way.

"You can do more than praying after you have prayed. You can never do more than praying before you have prayed."

After our conversation we sing with a group:

Drop Thy still dews of quietness,
Till all our strivings cease;
Take from our souls the strain and
    stress,
And let our ordered lives confess
The beauty of Thy peace.

Lailani sings with us, and I know that her heart prays.

22

A Leper Colony

Little children, abide in Him; that, when He shall appear, we may have confidence, and not be ashamed before Him at His coming.

1 John 2:28

In Formosa is a government leper colony where a courageous missionary, Mrs. Dixon, does miracles. Before she went there the lepers had to take care of themselves and lived huddled together in the greatest misery. She brought new sleeping mats and put planks around the cots so that the rats could not easily reach them. Together with the lepers she built paths so that their wounded feet could walk with greater comfort. She convened committees from the lepers who were still able to help those who had no fingers left to cook for themselves. German nurses work there now, and many improvements have been made. There is now healing for those in the initial stages of the disease, for new drugs do miracles for them, but most of the cases are too far advanced. Life is made much happier by the provision of a library and recordings of good music. The cases of suicide are now much fewer since the poor lepers began to realize that there are people who care for them. The crown of her work is a church on the hill, where every day the Christians gather together.

I try to spend all my spare time working in the leper colony. At first I am scared. I fear infection. But when I see how the other people work without any fear, I am ashamed, and I visit the sick who cannot go to church. It is a joy to lead the meetings. There is a hunger for the gospel. When I speak about the ocean of the love of God in Jesus Christ their faces beam with joy. One man especially catches my eye because of his radiant countenance, although his face itself is repulsive—the disease has destroyed his nose. This man is one of the courageous witnesses for Christ and has brought more than fifty other people to the Lord.

On one occasion an evangelist was speaking to these lepers from the text, "Abide in Him; that, when He shall appear, we may have confidence, and not be ashamed before Him at His coming" (1 John 2:28).

He asked, "Are any of you afraid that if Jesus should come today you would feel ashamed?"

One man put up his hand—it was the courageous soul-winner.

"Why are you afraid?"

"I have done so little for the Lord."

What a lesson for so many Christians who do little or nothing to bring other people to the Lord. This man is a leper—a mortally ill man, but he does what he can, and he is so humble. When he reaches heaven many people will say to him, "You have invited me here."

When I leave the camp many lepers stand at the gate. They are not allowed to leave the camp. Some are soldiers who have a red cross on their uniforms to show that they have leprosy and are prisoners in the colony like the others. Every day when I go they wave their hands—some hands are without fingers—and sing, "Don't be afraid of what may come. Our Father cares for you."

23

Resistance

Faith brings us on highways that make our reasoning dizzy.

It is a joy to work in Formosa because the Chinese are more free and open than the Japanese. The people in Japan can take politeness to such extremes that often you do not know what they really think. They believe that the worst that can ever happen is to lose face, and they have the same fear for their guests. That is why most of the time they agree with everything said—just out of politeness.

The Chinese are different. They can be very impolite.

At a theological school I say something that irritates the students. I tell them that it is all wrong to be studying theology without believing the gospel. I show them the danger of teaching the Word of God without having faith in it themselves. It may be that on God's judgment day we will find that those who have taught without faith have led many souls astray and have much to answer for.

A whole row of students take their books at that moment and begin ostentatiously writing to show very clearly that they are no longer willing to listen.

This is the last of my lectures in this school, and it is

a failure. Have I done wrong? Can God perhaps hit straight with a crooked stick and bless His Word even when it is taught by unbelievers? If only I could have another opportunity to speak. During that week I pray a great deal for the students.

One morning the telephone rings.

"We have been waiting for a speaker, but it seems that he is unable to come. Will you take his place in the theological school?"

Here is the answer. I have just enough time to ask some of my friends to remain in prayer for as long as I shall be speaking.

When I get there I take the bull by the horns and say, "Gentlemen, you have clearly shown me that you did not agree with my last lecture. Will you please be polite enough not to start reading or writing, but to listen to what God has to tell you? Pray that He will speak, and that the Holy Spirit will work so that all of us can understand not what Corrie ten Boom has to say, but what He has to say."

And now the Lord gives me a message. It is not weaker than the last one. I do not take back what I said, but there is more love and understanding in my words. I see that everyone listens, and there is a great blessing.

"The Bible is not like other books. It is the Word of God, the sword of the Spirit. We must handle it with reverence. When we read and teach it under the guidance of God's Spirit, it is a sharp two-edged sword. Paul shows us this very clearly in the first two chapters of 1 Corinthians. He tells us there is a difference between faith knowledge and sense knowledge. What we see by faith is an invisible reality, much more important than our logical thinking. Faith brings us onto highways that make our reasoning dizzy. Just imagine a captain who is unable to believe in his radar and is unwilling to use it in navigating, but instead depends upon his own eyes and what they can see. His ship would be involved in a severe collision in foggy weather. The foolishness of God is so much more important than the wisdom of the wise.

"Bringing the gospel is the Holy Spirit speaking through us. Whoever comes to God must believe that He is. Even psychology shows us that it is impossible to teach the gospel without believing in it. A good businessman has faith in his products. A doctor believes in the drugs he prescribes; and it is still more important that God's Word brings us into holy territory. We cannot play God's music if we are not tuned in by the Holy Spirit to His heavenly harmony. The Lord Jesus says, 'Except a man be born again, he cannot see the kingdom of God.'"

What a joy that God answers prayers, and that He gave me this extra hour. After the lecture there is a blessed discussion, and I know that God will perform what He began to do that morning.

24

No Unequal Yoke

It is costly to accept, but it is far more costly to reject.

Two girls come to me for advice, and they tell me their difficulties.

One says, "I am a Christian. My parents are Buddhists. When they go to the temple to worship at the shrine they expect me to go with them. I do not believe in Buddha, and I want to know if it is wrong for me to go with them without believing in what they say there. I go to make my parents happy and do not believe it can do me any harm."

I pray for wisdom and then tell her, "The Lord Jesus has bought you with His blood—a high price. He has a legal right to possess you wholly. You can never make a compromise with Him. He Himself says, 'No man can serve two masters.' Do you lose something by accepting that? Yes, it means that for Jesus' sake you lose your life, but you win a far better life. Is it costly to accept? Yes, but it is far more costly to reject."

The other girl tells me of an almost greater conflict. "I am engaged to be married to a Buddhist. He thinks it is all right for me to follow Jesus. He allows me to go to church and has promised me that when we are married he will give me complete freedom. What do you think of that?"

"The Bible says it is not possible to be unequally yoked with an unbeliever. Do you know what an unequal yoke is? Two animals of unequal strength put together to pull a cart are dragging against each other in an unequal yoke, and that makes suffering for both. It is really an impossibility. The Lord Jesus makes Himself very clear in this. Those who will follow Him must belong to Him and follow Him in everything. He who loses His life for Jesus' sake has Him as Lord and King in every part of his life and is, therefore, a yokefellow with Jesus. What riches! With Him we are more than conquerors."

After we have prayed together, both the girls surrender their whole lives into the hands of the Savior—an absolute surrender.

A month later, I meet a sister of one of these girls in Hong Kong. She tells me, "Since their surrender both of the girls are so intensely happy. Their letters are full of joy. One wrote to say that she has told her fiancé she cannot marry him, and there is now a great peace in her heart."

What is total surrender? A joyful experience.

And shall I pray Thee change Thy will,
    O Father,
Until it is according unto mine?
But no, Lord, no, that never shall be.
Rather I pray Thee, blend my human
    will with Thine.

His yoke is easy. His burden is light.

He knows, He loves, He cares,
Nothing this truth can dim,
He gives the very best to those,
Who leave the choice to Him.

Eugenia Price writes, "I have found that Jesus Christ never asks us to give up a single thing which He doesn't replace with good measure, pressed down and running over."

A man saw his little boy carrying a load far too heavy for him. He took in one hand the load and in the other hand the little boy.

Total surrender is like that—safe in the hands of Jesus.

25

Martyrdom

As thy days, so shall thy strength be.
Deuteronomy 33:25

Annie Flint composed this poem:

He giveth more grace when the burden
grows greater,
He sendeth more strength when the
labours increase,
To added affliction He addeth His mercy,
To multiplied trials, His multiplied peace.

When we have exhausted our store of
endurance,
When faith seems to fail ere the day is
half gone,
When we come to the end of our
hoarded resources,
Our Father's full giving is only begun.

His love has no limit, His grace has no
measure,
His power has no boundary known unto
men,

For out of His infinite riches in Jesus,
He giveth, and giveth, and giveth again.

How much will we Christians have to suffer for our faith? The Chinese of Formosa talk about the martyrdom of Christians on the mainland of China, and on that day I speak on Matthew 5:11 and 12, "'Blessed are ye, when men shall revile you, and persecute you. . . . Rejoice, and be exceeding glad: for great is your reward in heaven: for so persecuted they the prophets which were before you.' There is just one condition for strength for martyrdom, and that is to be filled with the Holy Spirit. Do not fear the future. Live for the moment. 'As thy days, so shall thy strength be' (Deuteronomy 33:25). When we are filled with the Holy Spirit He gives us all the power and grace we need for the present moment."

I see some with very unhappy faces as if they doubt what I say.

"Perhaps it will help you when I tell you some of my own experiences. During World War II, I was in a prison camp in Germany where the Bible was a forbidden book. It was only by a miracle that I was able to smuggle my Bible into the camp. When they searched us, I prayed to God to send angels to surround me, and although the woman in front of me and my sister behind me were both searched, I was not seen. This happened twice.

"When I entered the prison barracks I saw that one thousand four hundred people were to be housed in a place built to accommodate four hundred. It was indescribably filthy, and soon there were many lice. This was a disaster in itself, but at the same time it all worked together for good, for the guards and officers would never come into our barracks, as they were afraid of getting lice from us. Consequently, we were able to have a Bible talk twice a day. For that purpose, God used angels and lice! God can use everything. And what a privilege it was to bring the happy Word of God to those poor despairing people—to tell them of Jesus Christ who had broken the vicious circle of sin and death when He died for us, and that He now lives for us.

"Once we were assigned a new forewoman, a fellow-prisoner who had to keep discipline in the barracks. Her name was Loni. She was a cruel woman who always had a leather belt in her hand with which to beat us, and she reported to the officers all we did. One day, when I opened my Bible, my friends whispered, 'Be careful; Loni is sitting behind you. If she sees your Bible, she will tell the guard, and then you will certainly be sent to the bunker.' The bunker was a cell from which people never came out alive. 'O Lord,' I prayed, asking for wisdom, 'You know that we cannot live without the light of Your Word in this dark prison. Protect us from Loni. Grant that she doesn't take away our Bible or tell the officers that we have one.' That prayer gave me the courage I needed. I read the Bible, prayed, gave my talk, and after that we sang 'Commit thy ways unto the Lord,' a Dutch hymn.

"When we had finished singing we heard a voice, 'Another song like that.' It was Loni. She had enjoyed the singing, and we sang more on that day than we had sung on any day before. Later, I was able to talk with her, and show her the way of salvation. That was a happy ending.

"But I am no heroine. When you know that every word you say can mean a cruel death, then every word is as heavy as lead; but never before or since have I felt such joy and peace in my heart. God gave me grace to be a martyr. I do not at this moment need grace to be a martyr—I need only grace to speak to you and not be afraid of the spider that is sitting on the wall behind me and that I hope will not creep into the sleeve of my coat." (Formosa has remarkably big spiders.) "But that I know from experience—if tomorrow, or next year, God should call upon me to be a martyr, He would give me all power and grace."

With my story, the ice is broken, and now several Formosans speak up. One says, "Once there were ten Chinese who were to be shot because they had courageously witnessed for Jesus Christ. Before the captain gave the command to shoot he said, 'If any of you want to save your lives, just renounce Jesus.' One Chinese stepped forward and renounced Jesus. Many people were watching, and immediately one of them jumped into the place where the man had been standing.

"'What's the meaning of this?'

"'I saw a crown falling, and I picked it up,' the Christian replied.

"Then came the command, 'Fire!' Ten Chinese fell dead."

"Ten Chinese got martyrs' crowns," I commented, "and this is the greatest honor for a child of God."

It is as if a beam of light has made the darkness disappear. We go on talking about the honor of martyrdom. There is no fear left. The Holy Spirit has opened our eyes.

I look forward; God sees all the future,
The road that short or long will lead me
        home;

And He will face with me its every trial,
And bear with me the burden that may
     come.

After the meeting an old woman says, "The spider is not in your sleeve; he disappeared into that hole in the wall."

26

God's Embroidery

There is nothing too great for His power,
There is nothing too small for His love.

In New Zealand are many immigrants from Holland. The first years are often difficult, especially for the unmarried ones. Family life has an even greater importance in this country than in the Fatherland, where there are so many other things to fill their lives. No Hollander at home can imagine the loneliness of life on the farms.

At a meeting I have spoken about answered prayers. The evening is warm, and before we go to bed we sit outside and have a little talk.

A young immigrant asks, "Can you really trouble God with the petty things of your life? I dare to speak with God about my soul, but I carry the sorrows of every day alone."

"Have you ever thought what God's love for us means? Love demands love, and don't you think that we can make God's father-heart happy by showing Him our love in telling Him of our cares? Earthly parents are happy when their children expect much from them. In Psalm 147:11 it says, 'The LORD taketh pleasure in those that hope in His mercy.' Don't forget that God sees our sorrows through our eyes. Imagine a little girl who comes crying to her mother because her doll is broken. Her mother doesn't say, 'Come along, don't be silly; that doll isn't worth a penny. What nonsense to cry about it.' No, she understands perfectly that the doll is the little one's sweetheart, and she tries to comfort her and says, 'Let us have a look and see if we can mend the doll.' Because she loves, she sees the catastrophe through the eyes of the child. God loves us more than an earthly father or mother. And His love makes our problems great in His eyes and small in our eyes.

"I will tell you something that happened when I was a prisoner in a concentration camp with my sister Betsie. One morning I had a terrible cold, and I said to Betsie, 'What can I do; I have no handkerchief.'

"'Pray,' she said. I smiled, but she prayed, 'Father, Corrie has got a cold, and she has no handkerchief. Will You give her one in Jesus' name? Amen.'

"I could not help laughing, but as she said 'Amen,' I heard my name called. I went to the window, and there stood my friend who worked in the prison hospital.

"'Quickly, quickly! Take this little package; it is a little present for you.' I opened the package, and inside was a handkerchief.

"'Why in the world did you bring me this? Did I ask you for it? Did you know that I have a cold?'

"'No, but I was folding handkerchiefs in the hospital, and a voice in my heart said, "Take one to Corrie ten Boom."'

"What a miracle! Can you understand what that handkerchief told me at that moment? It told me that in heaven there is a loving Father who hears when one of His children on this very small planet asks for an impossible little thing—a handkerchief. And that heavenly Father tells one of His other children to take one to Corrie ten Boom. We cannot understand, but the foolishness of God is so much higher than the wisdom of the wise. With God, proportions are so different from ours. Perhaps in His eyes New Zealand is just as unimportant as a handkerchief. Perhaps in His eyes a handkerchief is just as important as New Zealand. I don't know. But this I do know: God answers prayers, and God's promises are a greater reality than our problems.

"Does God always grant us what we ask for in prayer?

"Not always. Sometimes He says no. That is because God knows what we do not know. God knows all. Look at this piece of embroidery. The wrong side is chaos. But look at the beautiful picture on the other side—the right side.

> My life is but a weaving, between my
>   God and me,
> I do not choose the colors, He worketh
>   steadily.
> Ofttimes He weaveth sorrow, and I in
>   foolish pride,
> Forget He sees the upper, and I the
>   underside.
> Not till the loom is silent, and shuttles
>   cease to fly,
> Will God unroll the canvas and explain
>   the reason why.
> The dark threads are as needful in the
>   skillful Weaver's hand,
> As the threads of gold and silver in the
>   pattern He has planned.

"We see now the wrong side; God sees His side all the time. One day we shall see the embroidery from His side and thank Him for every answered and unanswered prayer. But even now, God gives us an answer in the Bible so that we can see His pattern in the great lines. For instance, to those who love God, all things work together for good. Faith is like radar that sees straight through the fog; the reality of things at a distance that the human eye cannot see.

"When I was in a prison camp in Holland during the last World War I often prayed, 'Lord, never let the enemy put me in a German concentration camp.' God answered no to that prayer, but in the German camp we were among many prisoners who had never heard of Jesus Christ. If God had not used Betsie and me to bring them to Him, they would never have heard of Him. Many of them died, or were killed, but many died with the name of Jesus on their lips. They were well worth all our suffering, even Betsie's death. To be used to save souls for eternity is worth living and dying. In that way we saw God's side and could thank Him for the unanswered prayer.

"The joyful thing is that all the time we have to fight the fight of faith, God sees His side of the embroidery. God has no problems concerning our lives—only plans. There is no panic in heaven. And I surely believe that one day when we are with the Lord we shall look back over the ages and see the whole world's history. Then we shall see and understand God's pattern for this world, but already, even now, God has allowed us to know His plan.

"In Ephesians 1 we read, 'God has allowed us to know the secret of His plan, and it is this: He purposes in His sovereign will that all human history shall be consummated in Christ, that everything that exists in heaven or earth shall find its perfection and fulfillment in Him. And here is the staggering thing—that in all which will one day belong to Him, we have been promised a share' (PHILLIPS).

"In England there was once a king who was to be crowned. He asked, 'Where will my bride stand during the coronation?' The answer was, 'It is the tradition that your bride may not stand beside you.' The king replied, 'I will not be crowned without her.'

"Do you know that of the coronation day of the King of kings, Jesus says the same? 'I will not be crowned without my bride.'

"That is the staggering thing, that in all which will one day belong to Him, we have been promised a share. The best is yet to be."

27

⊶∞⊷

Travel Adventures

Where He leads me I can safely go,
And in the blest hereafter I shall know
Why in His wisdom He hath led me so.

One takes no risk trusting God; trusting man can at
times be very hazardous. Hudson Taylor said, "Why
ask the help of impotent man, when we have an almighty
God?" Gloriously certain it is that my missionary jour-
neys, my retreat in Bloemendaal, and my refugee camp in
Darmstadt all depend entirely on God. The message to
me has been very clear that I must never ask for money.
Often when I speak in churches, my hosts suggest an
offering, but I never request one. In fact, I warn those
who reject the message, whether it be a call to conversion
or a commitment to Christ, not to give money. Satan
sometimes suggests that an offering will satisfy God,
when in fact He is demanding our all. Losing our life for
Jesus' sake is an inescapable requirement. But how great
is our gain! We are the great losers when we persuade
ourselves that the giving of money is sufficient.

Hudson Taylor again reminds us, "We need not a
great faith, but faith in a great God." Is my faith then
always unwavering? No, indeed! It is Corrie ten Boom,

she of little faith, who finding herself short of cash in Formosa, turns her purse inside out at least three times and once again balances her checkbook.

Tomorrow I must make a short trip and pay the rent for my room. It is not a large sum I need, but it just is not there. Those very fine, helpful friends, shall I ask them? "May I not tell them, Father, that I need the money?" I pray. But the answer is plain, "Trust Me."

It is a busy day: three meetings and several talks with people. Tired out, I return to my room. My mail has come, twenty-six letters, the first to arrive in Formosa. There is not time to read them all now, but out of the first one I open falls a check for £50!

The next morning I open more letters. One tells of a Christmas offering so generous that I can travel halfway around the world. At the travel bureau I order my ticket. "Please arrange flights for me from Formosa to the Philippine Islands; to Auckland, New Zealand; to Sydney, Australia; to Johannesburg, South Africa; to Tel Aviv, Israel; to Barcelona, Spain; to Amsterdam, Holland."

The clerk, a Chinese woman, writes out my itinerary.

"What is your final destination?" she asks.

"Heaven," I reply.

"How do you spell that?"

I spell it out, "H-E-A-V-E-N."

She smiles and says, "No, I don't mean that."

"But I mean it," I retort, "but you do not need to prepare a ticket for me. I already have my reservation." She looks at me inquiringly. "About two thousand years ago the Lord Jesus died on the cross to prepare a place in heaven for me. All I needed to do was accept the ticket."

"That's true," says a Chinese man who happens to pass by. He is an employee in the office.

I ask him, "Do you have your reservation for heaven?"

"Indeed, I have," he replied. "I received Jesus Christ as my Savior, and He has made me a child of God. Every child of God has a reservation in the house of the Father."

"Then there is something for you to do. This young lady has no ticket. Please see to it that she does not come too late."

Again I turn to the young woman and say, "I experience great difficulties when I try to make flights for which I have no reservations. But you meet much greater difficulties if you have made no advance reservations for heaven. We are told in John 1:12, as many as receive the Lord Jesus, to them He gives power to become children of God. In John 14:2–3, Jesus says, 'I go to prepare a place for you. . . . I will come again, and receive you unto Myself, that where I am, there ye may be also.' You see, He even provides the transport."

When I get my ticket I see the route has been changed to Sydney, Tel Aviv, Johannesburg. The clerk explains there are no direct connections between Australia and South Africa. The stretch over the Indian Ocean is too long. "We need an island for landing purposes."

Laughing, I say, "Well, we'll have to pray for a little island in the Indian Ocean, for my route is Australia, South Africa, and then Tel Aviv."

Later she telephones me and asks, "Did you pray for an island? There is one after all. I have just heard that Qantas Airlines began a direct route between Melbourne and Johannesburg last month, and it uses the Cocos Islands, so you can follow your original travel plan."

When I arrive in Sydney I hear that the trip will take four days. All I need is packed into one bag, plus literature, notebooks, Bibles, and colored slides. I have taken colored pictures in many lands, and use them often in meetings. They are my most prized possession. The manuscripts with sermons and lectures are also very valuable to me. Though seldom reading my notes when I speak, I prefer to have them before me. I have been accused of ascending the platform with three Bibles and five notebooks, but it is hardly that bad. Meeting so many people, one hears a wealth of ideas, and I try to record as many as possible.

Walking toward the plane, a pilot offers to carry my bag. "That is too heavy for you. You can trust me; you will find it on your seat in the plane." But he heads in the wrong direction! He sees my anxiety. "Truly, madam, you can trust me. I'm just going to stop at the office. The bag will be on your seat."

But it is not on my seat! I check with the stewardess. We cannot locate the bag, but she assures me it has been stowed with the rest of the luggage. At Melbourne, however, I get a real jolt. A telephone message from Sydney announces that a bag belonging to Corrie ten Boom has been left behind.

"When can it be sent?"

"We can send it by plane to England, thence by plane to Italy, from there to Israel," and then a long list of stations and transfers from one airline to another. My precious bag! It is not even locked! It contains all my earthly treasures. I am unhappy and angry.

During the trip the stewardess and I have discussed what it means to be a child of God saved through Christ Jesus. A display of anger will scarcely be a recommendation, so I swallow my sharp words and try to say cheerfully,

"Well, it must be for some reason; nothing happens by chance." I am perfectly aware that this is no victory. It would be victory if I had no resentment at all.

The plane climbs and I prepare as well as possible for the night. How dependent one feels in a plane. I pray earnestly for protection and a safe journey. After a short nap I waken and unmistakably smell fire. The other passengers are also awake, and soon the stewardess comes and says, "I have good news for you. We're returning to Sydney to pick up your bag."

"Yes, indeed good news for me. But, tell me, are we not in great danger?"

"No. We're just having hydraulic difficulties. We'll stop for repairs while in Sydney."

Later it becomes clear what the hydraulic difficulties were. The mechanism that depends on the hydraulic system no longer functions. The landing gear has to be let down by turning a crank. The co-pilot stands before a window holding a flashlight. And every five minutes we are assured over the microphone, "There's absolutely no danger; we shall land safely."

I think, "Methinks thou dost protest too much," and am not reassured at all. Below is the sea. A plane, after all, is a very little thing. Where could we go in case of fire?

I am not afraid of death. Too often when a prisoner I had to face it. Moody said, "The valley of the shadow holds no darkness for the child of God. There must be light, else there could be no shadow. Jesus is the light. He has overcome death."

I pray, "Dear Lord, perhaps I shall see You very soon. I thank you for everything." My life passes before me as a panorama. How glorious to know that all my sins have been cleansed in the blood of the Lamb. "Promoted to Glory" was written in the death notice of a Salvation Army soldier. O death, where is thy sting? O grave, where is thy victory? I thank my God for the victory of Jesus Christ.

Then suddenly I think of the others aboard. Are they prepared to die? I pray, "Lord, spare us, prolong the day of mercy for those that do not know You yet. Let us land safely." Looking about me, it is remarkable how the others react. There is no sign of panic. But no one sleeps; all sit quietly in their seats. The ladies are busy applying lipstick or powdering their noses.

I ask the woman beside me, "Do you feel it is important to enter eternity with painted lips?"

"What do you mean?" she asks.

"We are all aware that if this fire continues our lives are in danger."

"Oh, it's just that I don't feel completely dressed if I haven't touched up my lips."

At that moment I feel an urge to stand up and say to the people around me, "Friends, perhaps in a few moments we shall all enter eternity. Do you know where you are going? Are you prepared to appear before God? There is still time to accept the Lord Jesus as your Savior. He died on the cross to carry the sins of the whole world, yours included. Believe on Him and you will be saved. He is able to grant eternal life." I know that I should say that, but I do not. In that critical moment I am ashamed of the gospel of our Lord Jesus Christ. There is fear of man in my heart.

I cannot say that we land normally in Sydney, but we all get out safely. We are delayed for two days, so rooms are secured for us in a good hotel. Now there is time to do anything we please. My bag is returned to me, but there is no joy in my heart. I am ashamed.

"Dear Lord, send someone else; I am not fit to be a missionary. With so many others I stood before the very portals of eternity and warned no one. Send me back home, Lord. Let me repair watches. I am not worthy to be Your evangelist."

I read on the margin of one of my notebooks something I had written down: "To travel through the desert with others, to suffer thirst, to find a spring, to drink of it, and not tell the others that they may be spared is exactly the same as enjoying Christ and not telling others about Him."

Later in the lounge a Jewish doctor approaches me and asks, "Do you know fear?"

"Yes, indeed. Very often I have been afraid."

"But you were not afraid tonight. I watched you all those hours we were in danger for our lives, but you were neither anxious nor afraid. What is your secret?"

A ray of light! Perhaps after all! I tell him, "I am a Christian. I know the Messiah, Jesus, the Son of God, has come. He died on the cross for the sins of the world, your sins and mine. We read in the Bible, 'As many as received Him, to them gave He power to become the sons of God,' and I have accepted Him. If our burning plane had fallen into the sea I had the assurance of going to heaven. Jesus has said, 'In My Father's house are many mansions: I go to prepare a place for you.' And not only has He died for me; He has also promised that in His name I have power to withstand the evil one. Whenever fear welled up in my heart this evening, I said, 'In Jesus' name, depart.' Even Satan gives way before that name. 'All power in heaven and in earth' is at the back of that name."

The Jewish doctor returns four times, and each time his request is the same. "Tell me more about Jesus."

Found worthy to evangelize after all! In this world to be acceptable we must pass examinations. God sometimes requires that we fail the examination, and only then will He use us. Paul says, "When I am weak, then am I strong" (2 Corinthians 12:10). Thus one learns that without Him one can do nothing, but "I can do all things through Christ which strengtheneth me" (Philippians 4:13).

The great sin of negligence I confess to Him who is faithful and just to forgive our sins and to cleanse us from all unrighteousness (1 John 1:9).

28

~∞~

The Old Boer

As victory is the result of Christ's life lived out in the believer, it is imperative that we see clearly that victory, not defeat, is God's purpose for His children.

In South Africa I am associated for a time with Dr. J. Edwin Orr. There is much I can learn from that lively, worldwide evangelist, with his great gift of teaching and his delightful Irish humor. I ask him not to arrange any meetings for eight evenings so that I may listen to him.

One night he speaks from 1 Corinthians 3:14: "If the work that a man has built upon the foundation will stand this test, he will be rewarded" (PHILLIPS). It is a strange experience, for he talks about me. He repeats what I had said, "'I hope never to return to Germany. I am willing to work in any part of the world, but not there.' And yet it was just there, where she had suffered in a concentration camp, that God sent her. She went; she brought her enemies the message of the forgiveness of sins, and also found many friends. Was she God's child while she was disobedient? So many fear they are no longer His children when as Christians they sin. When my boy disobeys me, is he not still my son? Fortunately Corrie did not persist in her disobedience, but went to Germany. Happily for her, or she would have missed her reward in heaven." Then he looks at me. "Come to the platform, Corrie, and give us your testimony. You get ten minutes."

Thus I stand before a large gathering of people, many of whom I later meet, and soon there are many invitations to speak.

One evening while speaking of the love we must bear our enemies, I tell the story of Carl. I can see by the faces of those before me that the Holy Spirit is at work. After the meeting a Boer comes to me.

"Fifty years ago I saw the British murder my children," he says, "and for fifty long years I have struggled against my hatred. Fifty long years I have tried to love my ene-mies, but never have I succeeded. Today I have seen the way. It is Jesus! What He has done for you He can do for me. He is the only One."

Had this been the only man for whom I had come to South Africa it would have been worth all the effort and expense. Jesus is the answer for South Africa with all its tensions and problems.

A meeting is held in a cottage in a Negro village. Young and old are packed into two small rooms. I stand in the doorway between the rooms and speak of Jesus' love and His suffering on the cross. A tiny girl of six supports the head of her sleeping baby sister as she sits on the bench beside her. The small rooms are hot and airless, and before long the little six-year-old also falls asleep. The little hand that bolstered the baby relaxes, and the baby tumbles to the floor with a bang, severely bumping her head. She screams at the top of her voice. Such a fall can be dangerous. It frightens me, and before I proceed, I pray, "O Lord, touch that little child with Your healing hand." At once the little one is quiet. Her father gathers her in his arms, and she goes calmly back to sleep.

29

Spiritual Pride

Most of us are cowards and compromisers. We will not face our sins. Christ came to lift us out of the old vicious circle of sin and death.

A young naval cadet comes to me with his difficulties. "Perhaps you can understand my trouble. My life is dark; I see no light."

"Tell me your problems. Perhaps together we can find an answer."

"To begin with, I never seem to know when to witness. One moment I speak up and spare no one, but an instant later when I should be witnessing, I am silent."

"You are a branch of the Vine. Imagine a branch that is cut off still trying to bear fruit. How foolish! You must be united with the Vine, the Lord Jesus, then He will bring forth the fruit."

"But how can I be in constant union with the Vine?"

"The Bible says, 'Be filled with the Spirit.' The Holy Spirit wants to live in your heart. 'He is ready to enter the heart of any child of God, just as light enters any room that is opened to it,' says Amy Carmichael. But there is no room for Him in a heart that is filled with sin. First you must have a clean heart."

"That's it exactly. For example, take my pride. I don't want to be proud, but there it is, always in my way. I am a minister's son, and because of that I feel I should really be a very good witness for Christ; but it is really my pride."

"Do you think your pride will disappear just because you wish it? Jesus died on the cross to deal with our sin problems. Look, I have with me a torch that does not light. I open it and pull out a piece of rag labeled 'pride.' Then others labeled 'worry,' 'discouragement,' 'inferiority,' also, 'adultery' and 'dishonesty.' Finally, a yellow one stamped 'hatred.' All these in beside the batteries—small wonder the torch did not work. All the rags must come out to make room for the third battery. Thus, only in a clean heart is there room for the Holy Spirit.

"How wonderful to have the answer to the sin-problems. 'If we confess our sins, He is faithful and just to forgive us our sins, and to cleanse us from all unrighteousness. The blood of Jesus Christ His Son cleanseth us from all sin' (1 John 1:9, 7). His blood does not cleanse excuses, only sins confessed. The two batteries in the flashlight represent conversion and rebirth. First, there is a decision we must make, the first battery. In John 1:12 we read, 'As many as received Him, to them gave He power to become the sons of God.' That is easily understood. Even an earthly lawyer transacts no business for anyone who has not shown enough faith in him to give him a commission. Then, when we accept the Lord, that very important thing happens of which He speaks: We are 'born again.' Born into the very family of God, the second battery. Then we are God's children.

"I could never be a princess of the House of Orange, though I were to spend millions, or study at a hundred universities. A princess is born a princess, and a child of God must be born a child of God—'Born again,' says Jesus. The moment we say yes to the Lord Jesus, the Holy Spirit performs the gracious miracle of the rebirth. The moment we are born into the very family of God all promises of the Bible are written in our names and signed by Jesus Christ. We have not to start at the bottom but at the height where Jesus finished at the cross.

"One of the riches inherited through these promises is that Jesus said, 'I will send the Comforter, the Holy Spirit, unto you'; and the most joyful commandment is, 'Be filled with the Spirit.'

"The third battery is the fulness of the Holy Spirit. We must confess our sins. He forgives and cleanses, whereupon we praise the Lord and give thanks. The Holy Spirit will fill every heart that is cleansed by the blood of Jesus.

"Look, there are now three batteries in the torch, and it gives light."

"That all sounds very wonderful, but during my quiet time I am always so busy with the sins I uncover that little time is left for praise and thanksgiving."

"That's another of Satan's devices, making us intro-spective. If we look within ourselves we are bound to find more and more sin. Paul advises us in Hebrews 12:2 to look unto Jesus the author and finisher of our faith. Why not pray with the psalmist, 'Search me, O God, and know my heart.' He will show you your sins. Not all of them at once, but increasingly you will recognize them, and always in the light of Christ's finished work upon the cross. Then God makes it very clear where you have to make restitution, and so you get right with God and right with men. To the end of our lives it remains a struggle against sin, but a victorious struggle. If only we put on the whole armor of God (Ephesians 6:11–18), we go from victory to victory. Clear the decks of your sins. Be filled with the Spirit and with the fruit of the Spirit which is love, joy, peace, longsuffering, gentleness, goodness, faith, meekness, temperance (Galatians 5:22–23)."

"I had more problems I wanted to talk over with you, but I see the answer now. I have lived like a beggar when I am indeed a King's child."

"Yes. We are what we are in Jesus Christ. God has 'made Him to be sin for us, who knew no sin; that we might be made the righteousness of God in Him' (2 Corinthians 5:21)."

30

<hr>

Truth Is So Simple

There is joy in the presence of the angels of God over one sinner that repenteth.

Luke 15:10

In the post office in Johannesburg is held a weekly Bible meeting. The walls of the beautiful lecture room resound to the music of Christian hymns. Christians meet there together and invite all their workmates; a tremendous chance for the gospel. I find it to be the same in many towns in South Africa, Christians also gathering in railway buildings and insurance offices during lunch hours.

After I have spoken, a girl who has a free afternoon brings me home. In the car we talk about the meeting.

"Do you know," she says, "I go every week to the lunch hour meeting and listen with great interest, but I have never made the decision to become a Christian."

"Have you time to stop for a moment near the kopje? I would like to show you something in my Bible."

We park in the shade of a tree. I open the Bible and read Isaiah 53:6: "'All we like sheep have gone astray; we have turned every one to his own way.' Have you gone God's way or your own?"

"My own way."

"We have all done that, but it is good that you know it. If you didn't know it, I could hardly give you advice. Now read on, 'The Lord hath laid on Him the iniquity of us all.'"

I take a book in my right hand and lay it on my left.

"Look, God has taken your sins and laid them on His Son, Jesus Christ, just as I have laid this book on my left hand. This morning you heard how Jesus died on the cross to carry the sins of all of us—the Lamb of God that taketh away the sins of the world."

We read together John 1:12, "As many as received Him, to them gave He power to become the sons of God, even to them that believe on His name."

"Now, what is written there? Does He give the power to become a child of God to those who try to be good and live a better life, or to those who are members of a church? No, only to those who receive Jesus. I say again, will you receive Him now? Jesus finished all that had to be done to make the barrier of sin disappear. Because of that God will forgive you."

She closes her eyes and prays, "Lord Jesus, will You forgive my sins? I receive you now as my Savior and Lord."

"Now we will read John 1:12 again. What are you now?"

"A child of God," she replies.

"Will you thank Him for that?"

Again she closes her eyes, "Thank you, Lord Jesus, for saving me, and making me a child of God." Then she says, "What a joy now that I know it for sure. I really feel that I am now God's child."

"How often I have experienced that when we praise

and give thanks the Holy Spirit witnesses with our spirit that we are children of God. This is a joyful beginning for you. Now go forward. Read your Bible faithfully. It is your book—about you and written for you. Confess all your sins to Him who will forgive and cleanse you. Not just sins in general, but mention the ones that the Lord shows you.

"The next thing is to join a church. This is not the foundation, for you are a child of God because you have accepted Jesus, but we need nourishing, teaching, and fellowship with other children of God. The Bible says in Hebrews 10:25: 'Not forsaking the assembling of ourselves together, as the manner of some is,' or as Phillips's translation puts it, 'Let us not hold aloof from our church meetings, as some do.'"

On the way home she says, "How simple the way is, really."

"Yes. Complications are put there by you and me and the devil. The truth is simple but so deep that we need the Holy Spirit to see the truth in its simplicity."

31

Gossiping

It is just as bad to be drunk with gossiping as with liquor. Gossip is the most insidious of all the compensations for an inferiority complex. It is not only a sin—it is paranoid.

In a students' summer camp, we sit together to talk over the day. It is really time to go to bed, but the evening is hot. Above the lake the crescent moon shines. The Southern Cross is just above the horizon. Some of the constellations are the same as we see in Holland, but their angles are a little bit different.

We talk over the happenings of the day, and a witty student criticizes the speakers of the conference. Her remarks are so accurate that we have to agree with her, and there is a lot of banter, but at the same time something of the joyful day is spoiled.

Sitting next to me is Shirley, a quiet and rather nervous girl. We don't really know her yet, but now, when there is a lull in the conversation, I ask her a question in order to distract the others from their negative talking.

"Tell us something of your life, Shirley."

She waits a moment, and it almost seems as if she is too shy to speak. But then she starts to talk.

"You know, I never planned to study law. When I was a child, my ideal was to be a nurse, and I went to a big hospital as a student. In our spare time we often went to a nearby beach. I always felt myself to be the least of all those clever nurses, and I had the terrible feeling that everything I said and did was wrong. I could not get myself in tune with the others. Many of them would talk about other people, saying how boring or difficult the patients were, and heavily criticizing the older nurses, and they always had something shocking to say about the moral lives of the doctors.

"One day they asked my opinion of a newly arrived student nurse. I was flattered at being asked and told them all the stupid things that the poor girl had done during her first week in the hospital. Suddenly I realized that everyone was listening to me; I exaggerated here and there so that my gossip became slander. But I was successful in gaining their attention and a little limelight. One of the girls said, 'Say, mouse, there is more behind that quiet face of yours than I had thought.'

"The next day I was working with the newcomer, and I saw many more of her mistakes and faults. Sometimes my friends of the beach looked at me knowingly when she did something stupid. For six weeks things went all right—no, I must say all wrong. I became more popular, and the new girl more nervous, and after a very sharp reprimand from one of the older nurses she left and went home; later she became a patient in a mental institution. After she had gone I really understood what a terrible wrong I had done. I decided I would never again speak negatively, but I could not row against the tide in the hospital, so I left and decided to study law."

"I fear that you will be a bad lawyer if you are always

going to speak positively and never negatively," says one of the boys.

"I am not afraid of that. It is one thing to see something wrong and to fight it with a positive purpose, and quite another to talk of wrong things in order to become popular and help the ego a little."

The conversation becomes general. I tell them how years ago in a girls' summer camp the atmosphere was almost spoiled by the campers because of their negative talking about each other. So we made a camp rule that before saying something negative we had to mention ten virtues of the person concerned. Sometimes it was impossible to find ten virtues, and so the negative thing could not be told. In the event of being able to find ten virtues, we would be so impressed at having done so that it seemed a pity to mention the negative at all!

One student tells us that in her campus, if anyone gossiped during meals, someone would say, "Pass the salt." Those were the code words to warn people that gossip was abroad. This idea is very simple and practical.

After that a boy reads from Romans 14: "Welcome a man whose faith is weak, but not with the idea of arguing over his scruples. . . . After all, who are you to criticize the servant of somebody else, especially when that somebody else is God? It is to his own Master that he gives, or fails to give, satisfactory service. And don't doubt that satisfaction, for God is well able to transform men into servants who are satisfactory. . . . Why, then, criticize your brother's actions, why try to make him look small? We shall all be judged one day, not by one another's standards or even our own, but by the standard of Christ. . . . It is to God alone that we have to answer for our actions" (PHILLIPS).

In Ephesians 4:30–32, Paul writes, "Let there be no more resentment, no more anger or temper, no more violent self-assertiveness, no more slander and no more malicious remarks. Be kind to one another; be understanding. Be as ready to forgive others as God for Christ's sake has forgiven you" (PHILLIPS).

How clearly the Lord Jesus tells us in His Sermon on the Mount, "Judge not, that ye be not judged."

One of the girls comments, "I am so thankful that we have spoken about these things. I have never seen so clearly that gossiping is just the opposite to what the Bible teaches. We would be afraid of stealing money from each other, but we don't think anything at all of stealing somebody's good name, and I don't know which is worse. What can we do to stop it?"

"I think that Psalm 141:3 gives the answer. 'Set a watch, O LORD, before my mouth; keep the door of my lips.' People who throw mud have always got dirty hands. You cannot whiten yourself by blackening others. Be patient with the faults of others—they have to be patient with you.

"Before speaking, first think: Is it true, is it kind, is it necessary? If not, let it be left unsaid.

"When you point your finger at somebody, remember the other three fingers point back at yourself."

32

Three Letters

> Those who criticise us are the unpaid guardians of our souls. If what they say is true, do something about it; if it is not, forget it.
>
> *Stanley Jones*

My program is not always clearly mapped out. The most important thing is to go where God guides. If the green light is showing, then courageously cross the street. If the light shows red, then wait obediently. Sometimes there are moments when I do not see the way. I am to attend conferences, but the dates are so arranged that I have two months free in between. I am in England and have not yet made many contacts. A minister invites me to go with him to his parish, which is one of those old English towns with many boarding schools. The invitation seems to be very attractive, as I can reach the same people for two months, join in the life of a parish, and learn from those who must always work in the same area. I thankfully accept the invitation.

On the first day there is no work, and being alone in my room, I find a very welcome opportunity for quiet time and Bible study. But at the end of a week there is still no work. I am unable to make any personal contacts. When any visitors come to the house my lunch is sent to me in my room. I do not know if there is really any activity in this parish—if there is I do not see it.

The minister and his wife are very kind, but I feel some opposition from them, and it is a strange experience for me to have to sit and wait. In many countries there is work for me. Sometimes the programs are so heavy that to answer all the invitations and fit everything in can be a real puzzle.

I search my heart to see if I am offended. One can so easily become too great to be used by God. One can never be too small for His service. Just then I receive a letter from a friend in Holland. He writes, "Corrie, your whole work is nothing but a flash in the pan. All this wandering over the world is just a means of finding adventure. You do so many wrong things that you lose the respect of other people, but that is what you deserve. The worst thing is that God's name is dishonored by your behavior."

Is this really so? How good it is that I have time to think it over and to talk with my heavenly Father about it. I am used to confessing immediately when I am aware of sin. It is so certain that when we confess sin we experience that God is true and faithful, and that He forgives us our sins and cleanses us from all unrighteousness, that I very seldom think of the past. But now I have a spring cleaning. I pray, "Search me, O God, and know my heart: try me, and know my thoughts: and see if there be any wicked way in me, and lead me in the way everlasting." When the Holy Spirit shows us our sins, it is always in the light of the finished work at Calvary. Sanctification is not a heavy yoke, but a joyful liberation.

The next day another letter arrives. This one is from a family with whom I spent a week as their guest—a retired prison governor from India with his two daughters. "God has so blessed your visit to us, that my daughters and I have been born again. Now all three of us are going to work for the Lord. I am going back to India, where I served the world for so long, and where in the future I shall serve God. I know the language of the Indians, and I will spend the last years of my life living with them and bringing them the gospel."

That evening I pray, "Lord, I am a branch of the Vine—nothing more, and nothing less. Give me tomorrow two souls to save as a sign that You can still use me."

The following morning the third letter arrives. It is from a young woman. She tells me, "God used your words to awaken me. I am now much more active. Today I had the joyful experience of bringing two girls to the Lord."

That is the answer. Indirectly God has used me for two souls. I can go on quietly. God works.

During the last week of my stay in the place the minister changes his attitude. He brings me into contact with schools, clubs, and a home for soldiers. The quiet time has gone, but what a blessing it has been. After this attack, I go on in greater dependence on Him who is our Vine. Without Him we can do nothing—with Him we are more than conquerors.

33

Ready for the
Second Coming of Jesus

The restless millions await the coming of the light that maketh all things new. Christ also waits, but men are slow and few. Have we done all we can? Have I? Have you?

C hanged people make changed cities; changed cities make changed countries; changed countries make a changed world," says a young minister.

We are at a house party in England. Many young people listen to his words. I look around me. Some people remain indifferent; others are full of enthusiasm. Is this the answer for the problems of our time, this atomic age, when the world is approaching the greatest crisis in history?

When I am alone with the young minister afterwards, I ask him, "Do you really believe what you said? I don't believe it is true. The time of grace is passing, and the world will not be changed by changed people. When the time of the Gentiles is fulfilled and Jesus returns, He has promised, 'I make all things new' (Revelation 21:5). I certainly hope that revival will come throughout the whole world, and that God will use it to bring in the fulness of the Gentiles, for revival is the true preparation for the second coming. That is why every Christian must be an evangelist as far as the opportunity is given to him by God. Then the coming of this time will be sped up. As it says in 1 John 3:3, 'Every man that hath this hope in him purifieth himself, even as He is pure.'

"It is truth that makes one free, not idealism. The expectation of the second coming of the Lord changes people from being earthbound to people whose eyes are focused on the future of the Lord, and gloriously opened to the great value of bringing the happy tidings to this poor world. They see that bringing people to Jesus Christ is the most important work for every child of God."

"I do not understand why you believe so strongly that Jesus is going to come again soon. Surely He comes into our hearts when we trust Him, and again in the hour of our death."

"The angel said differently. In Acts 1:11 it is written that when the disciples looked with amazement toward the clouds after the ascension, the angel told them, 'This same Jesus, which is taken up from you into heaven, shall so come in like manner as ye have seen Him go into heaven.' It doesn't say anything there about the coming of the Lord into our hearts or the hour of our death, but His coming on the clouds of heaven."

"All right; but so many before have expected His coming again. In crises throughout the world's history there has always been an escape for Christians in their expectations of Christ's return, and yet things have continued as they always have done from the start of creation."

"Peter has said exactly the same. In his second epistle, chapter 3, verses 3 and 4, he writes, 'Knowing this first, that there shall come in the last days scoffers, walking after their own lusts, and saying, Where is the promise of His coming? for since the fathers fell asleep, all things continue as they were from the beginning of the creation.' Search your heart. If there is a tendency to walk after your own lust, if there is love for earthly things, if you will not lose your self, your ego, then, of course, there will be doubt of the Lord's second coming. It is then that you will try to put forward logical and theological arguments. Study your Bible in obedience, and you will find many details.

"God's Word teaches us far more about Jesus' second coming than about any other truth, and it is about this that Christians know so little. That is partly the fault of the ministers, who perhaps mention the second coming in one sentence at the end of a sermon, or in the catechism once a year. But every Christian has God's Word, which can tell them very much about the future. The most important thing for a Christian to consider is his attitude, his being prepared. Jesus tells us about the wise virgins with oil in their lamps. Does oil here mean the Holy Spirit? When we are filled with His Spirit instead of love for our own lusts, then we are ready and can follow the advice of John when he says in his first epistle, "Abide in Him; that, when He shall appear, we may have confidence, and not be ashamed before Him at His coming' (1 John 2:28).

"I believe that God is opening the eyes of the theologians to the great importance of this truth. One of the atomic scientists told Professor Karl Barth that they are prisoners of science and politics, and asked him how the problem could be solved. Professor Barth replied that the only answer is the second coming of the Lord Jesus. He was right. When Jesus does what He has promised in Revelation 21:5, to make everything new, then swords will be changed into ploughshares, and atomic power will be used to build up instead of to destroy.

"Have you read my book *A Prisoner and Yet . . . ?* In it you can see that Jesus' light is stronger than the deepest darkness. Only those who have had the experience of being in a concentration camp can know how deep that darkness really is. No matter how deep down into darkness one goes, deeper still are the everlasting arms. The Czechoslovakian, Giorgiu, wrote a book after he had experiences similar to mine. Two people, both in a concentration camp; but that poor man had been there without Jesus Christ. I had Jesus Christ with me, and that made all the difference. He called his book *The 25th Hour.* In it he describes how he was once in a submarine where he was shown some white mice and was told that when the mice died it meant that the oxygen was giving out, and unless the submarine surfaced, the occupants would have only a few hours to live. Giorgiu writes, 'That moment has arrived in the world's history. The white mice have already died—it is a question of a very short time and then this planet will be finished. The day has twenty-four hours; we are in the twenty-fifth hour.' Is this nonsense, or is it true, that we live on a very dangerous planet where two or more countries have atomic bomb factories and worse? Henry Adams has said, 'We know so little, and our power is so great.' Are we really in the twenty-fifth hour? Now is the time for Christians to give the answer to a desperate world. The Bible is very clear in its description of the future. Those who read the newspapers and the Bible together know that we are approaching the time that Jesus spoke about. 'Look up . . . for your redemption draweth nigh' (Luke 21:28)."

"I know so little about the return of the Lord."

"That is a sure sign that you don't read your Bible. Do you know that one out of every twenty-five texts in the New Testament is about the future, and that the Bible gives many details? Frederick the Great has said, 'When you want to know how late it is on the clock of world history, look at the Jews.' It is very clear that a tremendous thing started with the Jews when the State of Israel was born on May 14, 1948. It is at the same time one of the oldest and the youngest nations in the world, and it is not only those who understand the signs of the times who realize that we are approaching the greatest crisis in history, but everyone in the world."

"But we have had times like that before. During the Thirty Years' War the Germans were preparing themselves for the second coming."

"Yes, but now things are far more serious than ever before, and look at the Jews."

"But, tell me, are you really not scared about the second coming of the Lord?"

"No. I know what to do with my sins. When we confess them, God is faithful to forgive us our sins, and the blood of Jesus cleanses us from all sins confessed to Him. Those who have the hope that Jesus is coming soon purify themselves as He is pure, and that is possible because we can bring our sins to Him. The Bible tells us very clearly how to wait for His coming. In Titus 2:13 it is written, 'Looking for that blessed hope, and the glorious appearing of the great God and our Saviour Jesus Christ.' Instead of looking for His appearing, too many Christians start arguing about it.

"But the millennium is mentioned clearly only once in the Bible."

"How often must it be mentioned in God's Word before you believe it to be true? But I don't mind what you think about the millennium. It is far more important for you to see the second coming as a joyful event for all God's children. In Revelation 22:17 John says, 'And the Spirit and the bride say, "Come." And let him that heareth say, "Come."' When these three agree, then He will come quickly."

"But I dare not say 'Come' as long as I am not sure if I am ready."

"Do you hunger and thirst after righteousness so as to be ready for that day? Then read on, 'And let him that is athirst come. And whosoever will, let him take the water of life freely.' God has prepared it. We have only to receive it. God's promises are available on demand. Read 2 Corinthians 5:21, 'He hath made Him to be sin for us, who knew no sin; that we might be made the righteousness of God in Him.'"

"One other thing. I dare not long for Jesus to return when there are so many unsaved people in the world. How terrible it would be for them."

"Do you really mean that? Then don't ask the Lord Jesus to delay His coming, but go as soon as possible to the unsaved, and tell them the way of salvation, for the most important work in these last days is bringing the gospel to everyone you can reach. The Lord Jesus, in Luke 19:13, says, 'Occupy till I come.' Paul tells us in 2 Timothy 4:8, 'Henceforth there is laid up for me a crown of righteousness, which the Lord, the righteous judge, shall give me at that day: and not to me only, but unto all them also that love His appearing.'

"You are concerned about those who are not ready. Do you realize that today there are more people not ready than yesterday; more children have been born all over the world than people have been reborn? So it is a little darker today than yesterday."

34

⦷⦷⦷

Translation of the Church

I do not wait for the undertaker, but for the Uptaker.

One morning, a woman reads in her Bible (1 Thessalonians 4:13–18 PHILLIPS), "Now we don't want you, my brothers, to be in any doubt about those who 'fall asleep' in death, or to grieve over them like men who have no hope. After all, if we believe that Jesus died and rose again from death, then we can believe that God will just as surely bring with Jesus all who are 'asleep' in Him. Here we have a definite message from the Lord. It is that those who are still living when He comes will not in any way precede those who have previously fallen asleep. One word of command, one shout from the Archangel, one blast from the trumpet of God and the Lord Himself will come down from heaven! Those who have died in Christ will be the first to rise, and then we who are still living on the earth will be swept up with them into the clouds to meet the Lord in the air. And after that we shall be with Him forever. God has given me this message on the matter, so by all means use it to encourage one another."

As she reads, it speaks to her in a special way. The signs of the times are clear, and that great events are due to take place soon is evident, not only to Bible readers but to all who read the newspapers. So deeply is she buried in thought about the Lord's return for His own that she has no ears for the doorbell. After a while it registers, and she opens the door, still holding her Bible.

The milkman is waiting impatiently. "You must be getting deaf, madam. I had to ring three times."

"I'm sorry. It is not that I am deaf, but I have just read something in my Bible so glorious I forgot everything else. Do you know that it is possible that some day you may come to my door and I will no longer be here? Also you many find every Christian home empty. I've just read that when Jesus comes again we shall meet Him in the air. We shall be suddenly changed, and then we shall see Him face to face. You may not realize why people everywhere are missing. Later you may hear, and ask, 'Why didn't that old woman tell me before?' That is why I'm telling you now. But listen, Mr. Milkman, if you accept Jesus as your Savior, you, too, will become a child of God and be among those who will meet Him in the air."

Whether or not we agree with the old lady's conclusions, we see that she knew what it meant to watch for the Lord's return.

"Can ye not discern the signs of the times?" (Matthew 16:3).

"When these things begin to come to pass, then look up . . . for your redemption draweth nigh" (Luke 21:28).

It will not be important that we have much money, but rather that we recognize at that reunion those for whom Christ sent us into this world, and to whom we have spoken of the way of salvation.

35

Zonneduin

The time is short—too short for listless
    dreaming
O'er vanished fancies fair.
Around the hearts are breaking, tears
    are streaming.
Thou art needed everywhere.

This evening a fresh breeze comes over the dunes and makes the air deliciously cool in the garden after the heat of the day. Although the sun has not yet set, I hear nightingales singing.

"How did you come to open this home?" an American visitor asks.

"My sister Betsie had a vision. She and I were in a prison camp in Germany where there were, among others, about one thousand Dutch people. She told me, 'God has said to me that we must help these people around us after the war. If they come out alive, they will find it difficult to find a way through life again. Their experiences here have affected their health, and there is a terrible darkness in the hearts of many—they are mentally sick. God will give us a beautiful house, with flowers and colors. There, many will find the way to life again. They will come in contact with the gospel and be found by Him who will be their Savior and Lord, Jesus Christ, and who has the answer to all problems. As soon as the house is opened we must travel over the world with the gospel to tell everyone who is willing to listen. We must tell them, too, that we have experienced that Jesus is Light in the deepest darkness.'

"Betsie died in the prison, but after the war I did what God had told her. Many Dutch people have been in this home—people who had been in prison or suffered in other ways from the war—but they are now back in their own homes again. It is now a home where everyone who needs a time of rest, or to spend a vacation, is welcome."

Zonneduin has become an international house. I have friends all over the world, and many come to visit Europe. Holland is so small that people can get to know the whole country by making daily excursions from this house. Close by there is a wood and dunes and a scenic reserve where many plants and flowers can be found. Bloemendaal is a beautiful place for walks, but a young Swiss girl tells me, "The most glorious thing for me is that here in Zonneduin I have found my Savior."

Holland is a beautiful country. There are countries where the scenery is mighty and expansive. Holland has its own special beauty. It is my Fatherland. It is not often that I am here, but when in Europe I try to come home for a time in between visits to other countries. I enjoy the far views of the fields, the blonde dunes, and the pine-trees of het Gooi, and in Zonneduin I have a room with my own pictures and paintings on the walls, and my own books in the bookcase.

"Why don't you stay here when you like it so much?" an English girl asks. "There is plenty of work for you here."

Before I answer, I am quiet for a moment and listen to the song of the nightingale.

"My life doesn't belong to me. I must follow where the Lord leads. I was bought at a high price and must be obedient to the One who purchased me."

"Isn't it costly to live like that?"

"Yes, but it is far more costly to disobey."

In my memory I see people in Bermuda behind bars, a tiny girl in Norton, a Boer in South Africa, school children in Cuba, lepers in Formosa . . . "We need your message; come back again," they have said.

My ability is very limited, but I am no more and no less than a branch of the Vine. Without the Vine I cannot do anything. Connected with the Vine, He gives His branches His nature, His victory, His love, His power. With Him, more than conqueror. Not good if detached.

"Go ye therefore and teach all nations" and "make them my disciples," says Jesus.

"Now to Him who is able to keep you from falling and to present you before His glory without fault and with unspeakable joy, to the only wise God, our Savior, be glory and majesty, power and authority, now and ever. Amen."

Conclusion

In Mexico I asked a boy, "Are you a child of God?"
His answer was, "Señora, I go to church every Sunday."

"That is good, but not sufficient. When I go into a garage, I do not become a motor car. A mouse born in a biscuit tin does not become a biscuit. There is only one way to become a child of God—obey John 1:12. Those who receive Jesus as their Savior and their Lord, He makes children of God."

"But my parents are fine children of God."

"God bless them, but don't forget that God has no grandchildren. After you have received Jesus as your Savior, you are adopted into the very family of God, and you can say to Him with a happy heart, 'Father, my Father' (Romans 8:15)."

The boy understood and made the decision that makes the angels rejoice.

And what about you who have read this book? Did you ever make this decision? If not, why not have a talk with the Lord Jesus and ask Him to enter into your heart? He has been knocking all the time you have been reading. And when you open the door He comes in (Revelation 3:20).

You are perhaps a faithful church member. But are

you sure that you are a child of God? When a young man and a young woman have fellowship there can come a moment when he asks her, "Do you love me, and will you accept me as your husband?" The young woman does not answer, "I like your morals, and you give me such nice presents, and I love to talk with you." When things are all right the girl says yes, and that is a decision for life.

Sometimes people answer me when I ask them to accept Jesus, "But I pray often, and I like the Sermon on the Mount." Do you think the Lord is satisfied with that? Jesus loves you very much, and that is why He wants your heart and the personal decision that is for time and eternity.

If you have, then read the Bible; it is your book, about you, for you. Learn the words by heart. "As newborn babes, desire the sincere milk of the word, that ye may grow thereby" (1 Peter 2:2). For the warfare of life you need the "sword of the Spirit." And that is the Word of God.

As well as memorizing Scripture, I strongly advise you to commence a Bible study course. These are two of the most helpful and practical ways of growing as a Christian. The Navigators have an excellent Scripture memorizing course as well as a Bible study course, both of which I can heartily recommend.

You will never regret that you accepted Jesus as your Savior and Lord. For ten years now I have traveled all over the world. I have met watchmakers who would have preferred to be farmers, and farmers who would rather have been watchmakers, soldiers who regretted not being in the navy, and sailors who wished they were in the army. I could go on and tell you about many frustrated people I have met. But never have I found any Christian who regretted having accepted the Lord Jesus as Savior. And you will not either. But now go on and take all the riches written on your name and signed by Jesus Christ.

He saves from the guilt, the penalty, the stain, and the dominion of sin.

How wonderful!

We are saved by the sovereign grace of God and the precious blood of Jesus.

How amazing!

He will make us instruments for the saving of others, that we might be to the praise of His glory.

How beautiful!

Jesus Christ opens wide the doors of the treasure house of God's promises and bids us go in and take with boldness the riches that are ours.

How great!

Jesus was Victor!

Jesus is Victor!

Jesus will be Victor!

Corrie ten Boom was imprisoned by the Nazis during World War II for harboring Jews. Upon her release, she began a worldwide ministry of preaching and teaching. *The Hiding Place* is the best-known book about her life.

A Note from the Editors

These books were selected by the Books and Inspirational Media Division of the company that publishes *Guideposts*, a monthly magazine filled with true stories of hope and inspiration.

Guideposts is available by subscription. All you have to do is write to Guideposts, 39 Seminary Hill Road, Carmel, New York 10512. When you subscribe, each month you can count on receiving exciting new evidence of God's presence, His guidance and His limitless love for all of us.

Guideposts Books are available on the World Wide Web at www.guidepostsbooks.com. Follow our popular book of devotionals, *Daily Guideposts*, and read excerpts from some of our best-selling books. You can also send prayer requests to our Monday morning Prayer Fellowship and read stories from recent issues of our magazines, *Guideposts*, *Angels on Earth*, and *Guideposts for Teens*.